JUDITH BAKER MONTANO

FLORAL
STITCHES

An Illustrated Guide to Floral Stitchery

© Copyright 2000 Judith Baker Montano
Developmental Editor: Barbara Konzak Kuhn
Technical Editor: Sara Kate MacFarland
Cover and Book Design: Rose Sheifer
Stitch Illustrators: Ginny Coull and Alan McKorkle
© C&T Publishing
Watercolor art and ink illustrations: Judith Baker Montano
Production Assistants: Kirstie L. McCormick and
Claudia Böehm
Photography: Judith Baker Montano unless otherwise
noted. Cover photograph and chapter-opener photography
by Chris Patterson.

Attention Teachers: C&T Publishing, Inc. encourages you to use
this book as a text for teaching. Contact us at 800-284-1114 or
www.ctpub.com for more information about the C&T Teachers
Program.

Library of Congress Cataloging-in-Publication Data
Montano, Judith.
  Floral stitches : an illustrated guide / Judith Baker Montano.
    p. cm.
  Includes bibliographical references and index.
    ISBN 1-57120-107-6
  1. Embroidery—Patterns. 2. Flowers in art. I. Title.
    TT773 .M57 2000
    746.44'041—dc21   00-010398

Published by C&T Publishing, Inc.
P.O. Box 1456
Lafayette, California 94549

Printed in China
10 9 8 7 6 5 4 3 2 1

TABLE OF CONTENTS

DEDICATION

To Ernest, my beloved husband...
our children: Kristin, Dana, Tara, Jason and
Madeleine...children-in-law: Jim, Eric,
Yoichi, Brenda, and Josh...our grandchildren:
Nicole, Rie, Gen, Kelse.
I love you all—you've given me the
only thing I need: a family!

ACKNOWLEDGMENT

Thank you to Barb Kuhn, my amazing
editor; Sara Kate MacFarland, my ever-diligent
technical editor, and Rose Sheifer, my talented
designer; to Gloria McKinnon and Faye King
of Ann's Glory Box; to Corrina Cox of
Peppergreen Antiques and Ann Riseborough
for the borrowed antique bits; to Phyl Drew
for floral research; and to Chris Patterson
for the Australian photo shoot.

INTRODUCTION

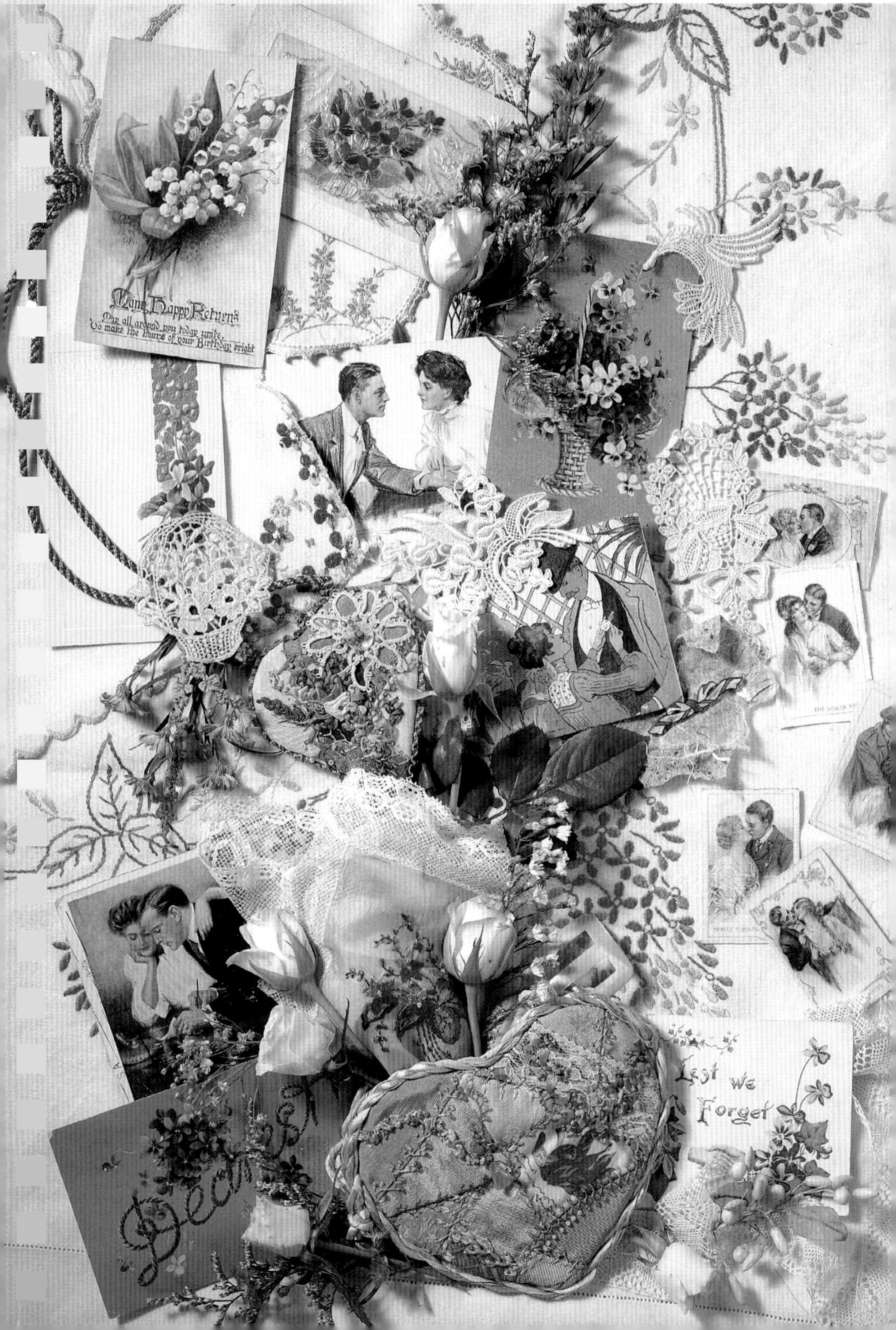

INTRODUCTION

lowers, gardening, and needlework are wonderful companions. Flowers are universal symbols of celebration, used for parties, parades, and weddings, so it is no surprise to see them worked in thread, ribbon, and yarn to enhance our surroundings.

I was born with a green thumb and a passion for gardening that was passed down by generations of family gardeners. For me, it is a most rewarding pastime and a wonderful form of therapy. When chaos and worries overwhelm me, I go to work in my garden. After digging, weeding, and planting, my life calms down, problems are solved, and I've reconnected with the earth, becoming grounded once again. My reward is a peaceful retreat filled with beauty and visual delight.

Gardening lets me examine flowers "up-close and personal." I can study shapes of buds, stems, leaves, and their shades of color. I make sketches and snap lots of photographs for research. Through my work in the garden, and as my embroidery and embellishment techniques have improved, I've gained the confidence to push them into another medium. Now I'm never afraid to experiment.

Many students ask me how to become more creative or how to combine the techniques they've learned over the years. My advice first is "Learn to do the technique properly, then you can get creative." For example, feather stitching on a crazy quilt has to be executed in a specific way to create beautiful, even stitches. Yet, it can also be distorted to look like seaweed or trees, but you must be confident in your stitches.

Picasso attended a formal art academy. After he mastered the traditional skills, he pushed the techniques into a new art form, and the rest is history. The same could be said for the alternative rock star who graduated from Julliard with a degree in classical piano. So practice and master your needle techniques, and then branch out, experimenting and pushing them into new effects. And, above all, have fun!

Floral Stitches is a dictionary of floral stitches and techniques to use in all avenues of needlecraft. It is a companion book to *Elegant Stitches*, and I urge you to use them together. I have tried to present new stitches, new ideas, and hints all related to flowers. Please enjoy!

CONVERSIONS

Over the years I have tried many different crafts and keep books on a variety of subjects for ideas and patterns in my mixed-medium pieces. I also keep magazines, clippings, photos, and slides, filed by category for easy reference. The following group of conversions will inspire you and get you thinking of ways to mix techniques and ideas.

My first step is to pick areas of my different samples and get them onto paper. Some of you will be afraid to try this but relax...you are simply trying out different design ideas.

Move the flower shapes around, trying different backgrounds. With tracing paper, transfer the drawing to heavier paper in order to color the design with watercolors, paints, or pencils.

I use a water-erasable pencil to trace my outlines. After dampening the chosen fabric, I paint the background with watercolor or dyes. When it has dried (I usually hurry it along with a hair dryer or an iron!); then I trace the details with a very fine pencil. I now have the fun of deciding what needlework techniques to use in my design.

 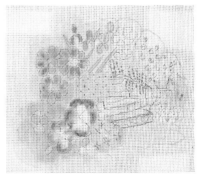

EMBROIDERY

Think back on all the stitches you have learned over the years (or refer to the Stitch Guide) and choose those that will best support your floral design. Remember that your fabric is like a painter's canvas, and you are the artist. Your threads and yarn are your paints. Use a good variety of threads and yarn to give the feeling of depth to the piece.

SILK-RIBBON EMROIDERY

Silk-ribbon embroidery uses traditional embroidery stitches but will add dimension and texture. It is a marvelous medium for floral designs. The traditional width is 4mm, and you must use either a chenille or tapestry needle to execute the stitches. The stitches are wonderful to mix with other embroidery techniques.

PUNCHNEEDLE EMBROIDERY

Always use a tight even-weave fabric for punchneedle embroidery, making sure the fabric is drum-tight in the hoop. The beauty of this technique is that the loops can be very long or short and can be sheared for a velour look (wonderful for the throat of iris, pussy willows, and Australian wattle). Punchneedle embroidery can be mixed with other techniques to create visual interest.

CROSS STITCH AND NEEDLEPOINT

If I want to transfer my design to a graph for cross stitch or needlepoint, I use a lightbox and graph paper placed over the watercolor design. (Be sure to use the correct size graph paper!) Then I color it in with watercolor pencils. Another method is to use plastic graph overlays, which can be purchased from craft and needlework stores. Lay the plastic graph over the watercolor design and then work it onto the chosen fabric. For the computer experts, there are programs that will scan your designs and produce a professional chart!

BEADS

A chart for beads is very similar to a cross-stitch chart. Once again, I first make a graph and work my beads according to color. I prefer to use beads for highlights, to indicate flower stamens, or to form fantasy shapes.

MIXED MEDIUMS

Floral techniques of all types can be used to create original and exciting projects. Now is the time to think back on all you've learned over the years from those classes, books, and techniques. Don't be afraid to combine them. Play around with color and shading. Relax and try different combinations until you come up with a pleasing design.

BACKGROUNDS

Nothing is more important than the background of your intended needleart design. Many things have to be taken into consideration, such as the mood you are trying to create, the contrast, and the workability of the material. Use color and tone to determine the mood. To give a soft, feminine look to your work, use light pastel colors on a background of white or cream. For an antique and muted look, use dusty colors on a taupe or grayed background. For sharp contrast and drama, use jewel-tones on black. Always remember that the background should not overshadow the needlework; it is there as a complement.

PAINTED BACKGROUNDS

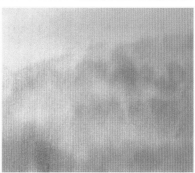

When you look at fabric as a painter's canvas, a whole new avenue of design opens up. For framed pieces, I use all types of paints (acrylic, oil, watercolor) but prefer watercolor. For large areas of color washes I prefer paint in tubes because I can work up larger volumes of paint. For anything that may be laundered, I use fabric paints and dyes. I apply these like watercolor washes. I dilute the paint, so I am forced to use several layers to achieve the finished look. Remember that a painted background is the background; your needlework should "float" on top. Decide on the finished size and cut at least one inch beyond on all sides. Tape the fabric (or pin) to a board so that it remains taut. Dampen the area you are painting (just as a watercolorist works on wet paper) to ensure the colors blend into each other. The paint will dry to a lighter hue, but be sure it is dry before you dampen and add another layer.

A painted fabric background works best if the base is a natural fiber and of a tight weave. The natural fiber (such as linen, silk, cotton) absorbs and holds the paint (polyesters tend to repel paint). The tighter the weave, the smoother the surface will be. Similar to choosing the rag quality in paper, a more textured surface might be exactly what you are looking for!

FABRIC TYPES

There are many fabric types that will give interesting and varied backgrounds. Always test to make sure the base is a natural fiber and that it is sturdy enough to act as a background for your design.

SATIN	Very elegant, formal fabric with a smooth surface. Test first to make sure the water does not eliminate the shine.
MOIRE	Fabric with a water-mark design...gives a Victorian, old-fashioned look.
VELVET	Another old-fashioned looking fabric...the texture provides added depth. Always choose velvet with a low nap.
MUSLIN	A coarser finish but a good choice...gives an informal feel, more of a country look.
SILK	Always an excellent choice. Can be shiny, matte, or a textured surface. Can adapt to any mood or look.
AIDA	Used for counted cross-stitch and has holes set at definite spacing. Good for mixed-medium pieces.

OVERLAYS

Use sheer fabrics as overlays to create interesting and unusual effects for the background. By cutting or burning the pieces into unusual shapes you can also create a feeling of depth and shadow. By layering several sheer fabrics, and letting the cut or burned shapes overlap in places, you can create light and dark areas for visual interest. A painted background may be

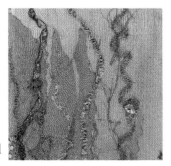

muted with sheer overlays to create a hazy effect. I use this last method to create underwater scenes.

Always have a good variety of sheer fabrics on hand. Look for organza, netting, tulle, and batiste. Many of these fabrics now come in a wrinkled state and some have glitter.

PHOTO TRANSFERS

As technology improves, we see more types of photo transfers. As opposed to those that were stiff and difficult to embroider, newer applications are soft and pliable. I still prefer the Australian photo method, but it requires a dry-toner copy machine that is becoming out-dated

(refer to page 161, *Elegant Stitches*).

Many antique paintings, Victorian ephemera, and photographs are now offered as designs to embellish. Although the finish is rather stiff, the base is very workable.

Today you may also scan artwork with a computer and transfer it onto fabric with a printer. This does bring up a point of concern: the subject of copyright. Become familiar with the rules of copyright and the restrictions.

Always protect yourself and always give credit where credit is due.

STAMPS

The variety of stamps offered today is immense...with the variety of fabric ink, the possibilities are endless. Try incorporating stamp designs into the painted fabric background.

THINKING LIKE A PAINTER

The process applied to successful needlework is no different than the rules applied to painting. I encourage my students to think of themselves as artists and to think like a painter and observe with a "painter's eyes."

Before you start, decide on the mood of the piece: where the light and shadows will lay, the time of day, and the light source. Always remember that lights come forward and darks recede. Large objects cast shadows. Just as a painter lays down layers of washes and paints, you will do the same with your chosen materials, building from the back to the front of your piece. Painting with paint, fabric, or threads is a backward journey! There are three major sections in a painting or needlework creation:

BACKGROUND	Everything in this area is very far away and small. It can be indicated by dark colors to show depth or by a hazy quality provided by overlays. Shapes in the background must be worked in fine threads and small stitches.
MIDGROUND	Everything in this area is of medium proportion. It is the separating area between "here" and "way over there." Some midground shapes should overlap objects in the background to create a feeling of depth. Work with medium-weight threads and lighter colors.
FOREGROUND	Everything in this area is very visible and more detailed. Work with heavier threads and in lighter colors to create depth and texture.

Garden scenes and landscapes require a bit more thought. Along with the background, midground, and foreground, you must decide on the horizon line (the distinguishing line between sky and land). The viewer's eye will always travel to the horizon line. A painting hint is to never put the horizon line in the center of your piece because it is very disturbing to the eye. Always put the horizon line above or below the center mark.

To make the eye travel within the design, use two painting techniques: the V shape and the S shape. For example, by creating a valley—a V shape—of trees and shrubs for a garden scene (in the center of the v), the viewer will instantly look into the garden area.

The S shape, whether a path, road, or stream, will draw the viewer's eye into the picture and grab his attention. As the eye travels along the S shape, the eye perceives the picture details.

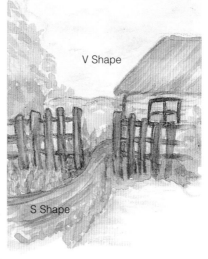

V Shape

S Shape

For garden and floral landscapes that include water, there are a few points which will make for a more pleasing and realistic picture. Large expanses of water always lie in a straight horizontal line and can form the horizon line. Smooth, calm water acts as a reflector, or mirror, and the upside-down reflected image needs to be indicated somehow. Little inlets and lagoons are shadowed. Remember that lakes and rivers are contained by banks of land, so the bank fabric must lay over the water fabric. The sea and ocean waters roll in and over the beaches, so lay the water material over the beach fabric!

One of the biggest barriers for my students to overcome is the use of color. Often their confidence has been eroded over the years, and they've been led to believe that color is some big mystery. I have a simple formula that helps to overcome these fears. The following Montano Color Chart is easy to follow and applies to clothing design, crazy quilting, landscapes, and all types of needlework.

MONTANO COLOR CHART

To follow this chart you must think like a painter. On the top row you see the word "paint". Let's assume the painter wants to paint a floral landscape, and she has to decide if it will be a light, medium, or dark value.

PAINT					
LIGHT		MEDIUM		DARK	
	LIGHT MED.		DARK MED.		
add white to paint	add a little black to paint		add more black	contrast between colors	

FABRIC					
PASTEL		DUSTY		JEWEL	
soft	desert		Rembrandt	Mardi Gras	
baby	hazy		antique	fireworks	
feminine	old		moody	dramatic	

EXTENDERS AND BACKGROUNDS				
white	cream		black	black
cream	light gray		dark gray	
	taupe		taupe	

HIGHLIGHTS				
silver	silver		silver	silver
			old gold	old gold
				rust orange

LIGHT: To create something with lots of light, a painter squirts out the basic colors and then adds lots of titanium white. The colors become very light and soft (red becomes pink, orange becomes peach, purple becomes soft lavender).

LIGHT MEDIUM: To create a desert scene, she adds a bit of black to the white to make gray, then adds this to her basic colors.

DARK MEDIUM: To create something moody, she will simply add more black to the paint in order to darken the piece.

DARK: Think of sharp contrast, lots of drama (perhaps fireworks or neon lights). Black always makes bold colors seem more vibrant.

FABRIC: In fabric and thread terms, light becomes pastel, medium becomes dusty, and dark becomes jewel tones. Try looking through your fabrics and threads to decide what category they each belong. Always keep in mind that lights come forward and darks recede.

EXTENDERS AND BACKGROUNDS: These are colors that will extend your work visually and work well for the background. They always complement and show off your chosen colors in the best possible way.

HIGHLIGHTS: These are colors that will add a bit of sparkle and interest to your work.

COLOR WHEEL

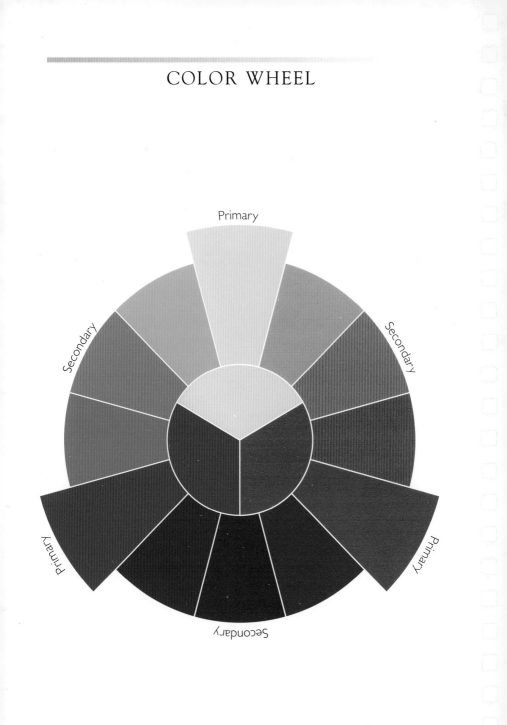

Primary

Secondary

Secondary

Primary

Primary

Secondary

Color Wheel Simplified

Please invest in a simple color wheel and learn how to use it. First look at the whole wheel and study the spectrum of colors. You will notice that there is a warm side and a cool side to the wheel (warm being reds and oranges, cool being blues and greens).

Look for the primary colors which are red, blue, and yellow. If these are mixed together you will get three secondary colors which are green, violet, and orange (yellow + blue = green; blue + red = violet; red + yellow = orange). Now there are six distinct colors that can be combined to provide six tertiary colors which are yellow-green, blue-green; blue-violet, red-violet; red-orange and yellow-orange. All of these colors are shown on the outside of the circle.

Complementary color combinations are what I use most of all. Look for your favorite color on the wheel and then look straight across it. This color is its complement. For example, the opposite of red is green. We see these two complementary colors used every holiday season. If you choose violet (purple) and look across to yellow, once again you have complementary colors. Study the wheel and find the various complementary selections.

If you want to use more than a set of complementary colors, look over the color wheel and choose a triad combination. These are three colors that are set apart equal distance on the color wheel. In a wheel there are four different combinations of triad combinations.

If you wish to use only one color, that would be known as a monochromatic color scheme. In order to give this extra interest you can use combinations of shiny, matte, and textured materials. Lastly, analogous color combinations are very harmonious because they are neighboring hues.

Framing Ideas

Framing can become very expensive, yet it is such an important part of the finished piece. You should always try to present your artwork in the best possible way. I try to economize costs by working in traditional sizes of mats and frames. Because most of my work is heavily layered, I use a double mat with a floater between the two layers.

1. Purchase the double mat and some foam-core board from your local art store. Lay out your materials: tacky glue, masking tape, fleece, scissors, the finished piece, and the inside mat. Set the outer mat aside.
2. Cut two pieces of fleece: one exactly the size as the inside opening of the mat and one ¼" larger all around.
3. Turn the mat over and glue along the inside edge of the opening. Glue the finished art piece into the mat. With tape, secure two sides, then pull the piece until taut; tape in place until all sides are secure. Set aside until completely dry.
4. Turn the mat over and lay the larger fleece piece directly behind the finished piece. Make sure the fleece edges overlap the edges of the mat.
5. Lay in the smaller fleece and make sure it lines up with the actual mat opening. Smear tacky glue onto the back of the mat and lay the cardboard backing in place.
6. Turn the piece over, pressing firmly until the padding in the back bulges. Lay a cloth over the mat (to protect it from smudges). Set heavy books atop the mat until it is completely dry.

7. Cut strips of foam core and glue along the front edges of the inside mat. Glue the outer mat to the strips. (Make sure the glass will not touch the artwork.) You may have to add more strips to make it deeper. Finally, take the piece to your art store for framing.

ne of the easiest ways to define flowers is by shape, but I've found that some flowers fit in more than one category. Here are sketches and photos from my many teaching trips and a list of stitches to use for each.

BERRY SHAPES

Berry shapes can be round or oval, smooth or pitted. Think about the shapes and how much detail you want to add.

Apple tree

Kumquat

Rose hips

Lilly-pilly tree

Queen palm

KUMQUAT
Leaves: Fishbone Stitch, Judith's Curled Leaf, Lazy Daisy
Stems: Feather Stitch, String of Pearls
Branches: Chain Stitch, Ribbon Split Stitch

LILLY-PILLY TREE
Berries: Chinese Knots, Colonial Knots, Raised Straight Stitch
Stems: Couched Threads, Portuguese Knotted Stem
Leaves: VanDyke Stitch, Fly Stitch Leaf, Fishbone Stitch

APPLE TREE
Fruit: Chinese Knots, French or Colonial Knots, Circle Buttonhole
Leaves: VanDyke Stitch, Judith's Curled Leaf, Fishbone Stitch
Stem: Chain Stitch, Feather Stitch, String of Pearls
Branches: Portuguese Stem Stitch, Chain Stitch, Wool Rosebud

ROSE HIPS
Fruit: Granitos, Bullion Rosebud
Leaves: Lazy Daisy, Judith's Curled Leaf, Fly Stitch Leaf
Branches: Feather Stitch, String of Pearls, Chain Stitch

QUEEN PALM
Berries: Granitos, Colonial Knots, Circle Buttonhole
Stems: String of Pearls, Portuguese Stem Stitch, Chain Stitch
Trunk: Chain Stitch, Outline Stitch, Satin Stitch, Crochet Chain Stitch, Ribbon Split Stitch

CLUSTER SHAPES

This is a huge category because clusters come in all shapes and sizes! The whole flower is composed of many small florets.

Snapdragon

Cassia vine

Queen Anne's lace

Hydrangea

Spiraea

SNAPDRAGON

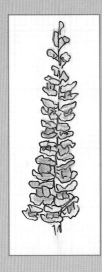

Leaves: Stab Stitch, Lazy Daisy with Bullion Stitch

Stem: Couched Thread, Stem Stitch

Florets: Judith's Curled Leaf, Joyce's Flower, Stab Stitch, Lazy Daisy

CASSIA VINE

Leaves: Fern Stitch, Fly Stitch

Stem: Stem Stitch, Couched Thread

Florets: Montano Knots, Stab Stitch

QUEEN ANNE'S LACE

Leaves: Stab Stitch, Lazy Daisy, Straight Stitch

Stem: Stem Stitch, Chain Stitch, Straight Stitch

Florets: French Knots, Chinese Knots, Fly Stitch

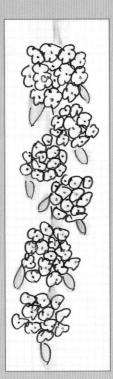

HYDRANGEA

Leaves: Sheer Ribbon Leaves, Judith's Curled Leaf

Florets: Ribbon Loop Flowers, Loop Stitch, Joyce's Flower

SPIRAEA

Leaves: Ribbon Stab Stitch, Judith's Curled Leaf

Stems: Couched Thread

Florets: Chinese Knots, French Knots

DAISY SHAPES

Ever-cheerful and fun to stitch, the daisy shapes can use many simple stitches. These flower shapes lend themselves well to thread, yarn, and ribbon.

Sunflower

Zinnia

Shasta daisy

Cosmos

Gerber daisy

ZINNIA

Leaves: Feather Stitch Leaf, Fly Stitch Leaf, Ribbon Stab Stitch

Stem: Couched Thread, Chain Stitch

Petals: Layered Stab Stitches, Side Ribbon Stitch

Center: Pistil Stitches, Chinese Knots

COSMOS

Leaves: Stab Stitch, Fly Stitch Leaf, Fern Stitch

Stem: Chain Stitch, Outline Stitch

Petals: Japanese Ribbon Stitch, Raised Ribbon Stitch, Lazy Daisy

Center: Chinese Knots, French Knots

SUNFLOWER

Leaves: Sheer Ribbon Leaf, Satin Stitch, Circle Buttonhole

Stem: Twisted Ribbon Tube, Ribbon Split Stitch

Petals: Ribbon Stab Stitch, Lazy Daisy, Japanese Ribbon Stitch

Center: Colonial Knot, French Knot, Chinese Knots

GERBER DAISY

Leaves: Sheer Ribbon Leaf, VanDyke Stitch, Fishbone Stitch

Stem: Couched Thread, Ribbon Split Stitch

Petals: Stab Stitch, Japanese Ribbon Stitch

Center: Chinese Knots with Loop Stitch, French Knots, Tufted Stitches (sheared)

SHASTA DAISY

Leaves: Japanese Ribbon Stitch, Stab Stitch, Long Lazy Daisy, Eyelet Stitch

Stem: Chain Stitch, Outline Stitch

Petals: Ribbon Stab Stitch, Lazy Daisy with Bullion Stitch

Center: French Knots, Chinese Knots

LILY SHAPES

Lilies come in many shapes and sizes, so you may use a variety of stitches. Lily shapes are so beautiful that I found it difficult to choose only five to share with you.

Water lily

Iris

Crocosmia

Easter lily

Belladonna lily

IRIS
Leaves: Japanese Ribbon Stitch, Long Lazy Daisy
Stems: Chain Stitch, Couched Thread
Petals: Judith's Curled Leaf, Side Ribbon Stitch
Center: Tufted Stitch

BELLADONNA LILY
Stems: Couched Thread, Chain Stitch,
Ribbon Split Stitch
Petals: Twisted Ribbon, Side Ribbon Stitch

WATER LILY
Leaves: Sheer Ribbon, Circle Buttonhole
Petals: Lazy Daisy with Bullion Stitch,
Ribbon Stab Stitch
Center: Ribbon Lazy Daisy with French Knot

CROCOSMIA
Leaves: Japanese Ribbon Stitch, Long Stab Stitch
Stems: Chain Stitch or String of Pearls
Petals: Side Ribbon Stitch, Stab Stitch
Center: Outline or Straight Stitch with
French Knots

EASTER LILY
Leaves: Lazy Daisy with Bullion Stitch, Stab Stitch
Stems: Couched Thread, Ribbon Split Stitch
Center: Straight Stitch with Granitos
Petals: Ribbon Split Stitch with Twisted Ribbon
Stitch or Side Ribbon Stitch

ROSETTE SHAPES

The flowers in this category are multi-petaled, with a lovely fullness to them. The buds are equally pretty.

Begonia

Gardenia

Peony

Marigold

Rose

BEGONIA
Leaves: Sheer Ribbon, Circle Buttonhole Stitch
Stem: Couched Thread, Ribbon Split Stitch
Petals: Twisted Ribbon Stitch

PEONY
Leaves: VanDyke Stitch, Fly Stitch Leaf, Lazy Daisy
Stem: Chain Stitch, Split Stitch
Petals: Jan's Rose, Helen's Rose, Side Ribbon Stitch
Buds: Granitos, Padded Bud, Lazy Daisy Bud

MARIGOLD
Leaves: Fly Stitch, Straight Stitch, Fern Stitch
Stem: Chain Stitch, Outline Stitch
Petals: Twisted Ribbon Stitch, Victorian Knotted
Pom-poms, Loop Stitch

GARDENIA
Leaves: Judith's Curled Leaf, Fly Stitch, VanDyke
Stitch
Stem: Portuguese Stem Stitch, String of Pearls
Petals: Jan's Rose, Helen's Rose, Ribbon Split Stitch
Buds: Lazy Daisy Rosebud, Judith's Curled Leaf
(overlapping)

ROSE
Leaves: Lazy Daisy, Judith's Curled Leaf, Feather
Stitch Leaf, Fishbone Stitch
Stem: Feather Stitch, String of Pearls
Petals: Wool Rose, Helen's Antique Rose, Jan's
Antique Rose, Folded Ribbon Rose, Tube Rose
Buds: Wool Rosebud, Folded Rosebud, Japanese
Wire Ribbon Bud, Lazy Daisy Rosebud

SAUCER SHAPES

Most of these flowers have beautiful centers within a cupped shape that can be adapted by many easy stitches.

Cactus

California poppy

Anemone

Lisianthus

Hollyhock

CALIFORNIA POPPY

Stem: Outline Stitch, Chain Stitch
Petals: Christine's Blossoms, Raised Ribbon Stitch
Center: French Knots
Leaves: Feather Stitch (overlapping), Fern Stitch

LISIANTHUS

Stems: Outline Stitch, Stem Stitch
Petals: Raised Ribbon Stitch, Stab Stitches (overlapping), Side Ribbon Stitch
Leaves: Lazy Daisy, Judith's Curled Leaf

CACTUS

Stem: (none sprout from cactus)
Petals: Mokuba Flower, Stab Stitch, Raised Ribbon Stitch
Center: Pistil Stitch, Chinese Knots
Bud: Granitos, Colonial Knots

ANEMONE

Stem: Couched Thread, Split Stitch
Petal: Helen's Antique Rose, Stab Stitch
Center: Chinese Knots with Loops
Bud: Lazy Daisy Rosebud
Leaves: Feather Stitch (overlapped), Long & Short Straight Stitches

HOLLYHOCK

Stem: Split Stitch
Petal: Circle Buttonhole, Ribbon Split Stitch, Raised Ribbon Stitch
Center: Colonial Knots
Bud: Colonial Knots, Granitos, Wool Rosebud
Leaves: Circle Buttonhole, Sheer Ribbon Leaf

STAR AND CROSS SHAPES

These shapes often overlap, which helps the stitcher when creating layers of floral shapes. Keep count of the number of petals.

Passion flower

Clematis

Clematis

Pansy

Frangipani

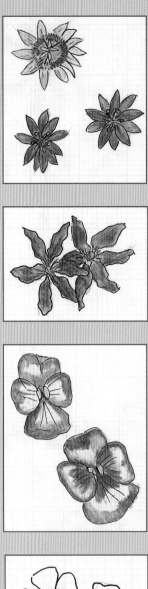

PASSION FLOWER

Stem: Couched Thread, Chain Stitch, Outline Stitch

Petals: Backstitch Spiderweb with Stab Stitch (surround), Side Ribbon Stitch, Drizzle Stitch, Twisted Ribbon

Leaves: Judith's Curled Leaf, VanDyke Stitch

CLEMATIS

Stem: Couched Thread, Chain Stitch

Petals: Drizzle Stitch, Side Ribbon Stitch

Leaves: Fly Stitch Leaf, Feather Stitch Leaf, Long Curled Leaf

PANSY

Stem: Outline Stitch, Chain Stitch

Petals: Wire Ribbon Pansy, Pansy Stitch, Victorian Velvet Pansy, Cast-On Stitch

Leaves: Judith's Curled Leaf, Fly Stitch Leaf, Circle Buttonhole

FRANGIPANI

Stem: String of Pearls, Feather Stitch

Branch: Portuguese Stem Stitch

Petals: Cast-On Stitch Flower, Five-Petal Gathered Flower

Leaves: Lazy Daisy with Bullion Stitch, Stab Stitch

TROPICS

The tropics are host to lush greenery, vivid color, and strange, exotic shapes. I like to use overlapping ribbon stitches and thread stitches for tropical flowers.

Gloriosa

Flame tree

Bird of Paradise

Orchid tree

Ginger

FLAME TREE
Stem: Couched Thread
Tip: Oyster Stitch, French Knot
Pistils: Long Straight Stitch with Beads
Petals: Japanese Ribbon Stitch, Drizzle Stitch
Leaf: Circle or Triangle Buttonhole

GINGER
Stem: Couched (heavy) Thread, Chain Stitch
Leaves: Japanese Ribbon Stitch
Petals: Ribbon Lazy Daisy (overlapping) with French Knot (overlapping), Side Ribbon Stitch

GLORIOSA
Stem: Chain Stitch
Petals: Twisted Ribbon Stitch, Japanese Ribbon Stitch
Stamens: Granitos, Small Bullions, Long Straight Stitch

BIRD OF PARADISE
Stem: Ribbon Split Stitch
Petals: Stab Stitch with Japanese Ribbon Stitch, Straight Stitches
Leaves: Japanese Ribbon Stitch, Sheer Ribbon Leaf

ORCHID TREE
Branch: Portuguese Stem Stitch
Stem: Chain Stitch, String of Pearls
Petals: Twisted Ribbon Stitch, Stab Stitch
Leaves: Sheer Ribbon Leaf, VanDyke Stitch

TRUMPET SHAPES

These flowers have a long neck and a frill that flares out like a trumpet. They are very pretty and fun to create.

Daffodil

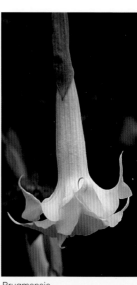

Brugmansia

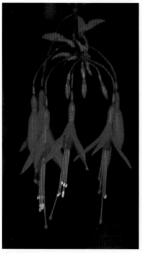

Fuchsia

Morning Glory

Carolina jasmine

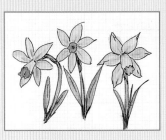

DAFFODIL

Stem: Chain Stitch, Couched Thread

Leaves: Japanese Ribbon Stitch, Lazy Daisy Stitch, Stab Stich

Petals: Japanese Ribbon Stitch with Judith's Curled Leaf Ruffle, Lazy Daisy

Center: Raised Ribbon Stitch

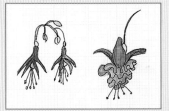

FUCHSIA

Stem: Outline Stitch, Chain Stitch

Leaves: Long Lazy Daisy

Petals: Japanese Ribbon Stitch, Side Ribbon Stitch, Gathered Ribbon Stitch

Center: Straight Stitch with Bead, Long Pistil Stitch

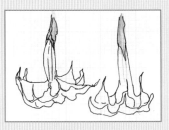

BRUGMANSIA

Stem: Couched Thread, Ribbon Split Stitch

Leaves: Circle Buttonhole, Sheer Ribbon Leaf

Petals: Ribbon Split Stitch with Twisted Ribbon Stitch tips

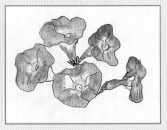

MORNING GLORY

Stem: Outline Stitch, Couched Thread

Leaves: Circle Buttonhole, Sheer Ribbon Leaf

Petals: Raised Straight Stitch with Stab Stitch base

CAROLINA JASMINE

Stem: Portuguese Stem Stitch, Chain Stitch

Leaves: VanDyke Stitch, Fly Stitch Leaf

Petals: Judith's Curled Leaf with Stab Stitch base

TUFTED SHAPES

These floral shapes always remind me of messy hairdos; they are really fun to make.

Stokesia

Liatris

Thistle

Spider Mum

Tassel flower

STOKESIA

Leaves: Lazy Daisy, Stab Stitch

Stem: Chain Stitch, Couched Thread

Petal: Twisted Ribbon Stitch, Stab Stitch, Japanese Ribbon Stitch

THISTLE

Leaves: Sheer Ribbon Leaf, VanDyke Stitch, Feather Stitch Leaf

Stem: Split Stitch

Petals: Tufted Stitch, End-String Flower with padded bud base

TASSEL FLOWER

Leaves: Stab Stitch, Lazy Daisy, Fishbone Stitch

Stem: Chain Stitch, Couched Thread

Petals: Tufted Stitch, End-String Flower

LIATRIS

Leaves: Stab Stitch, Japanese Ribbon Stitch, Long Lazy Daisy

Stem: Couched Thread

Petals: Tufted Stitch, Straight Stitch, End-String Flower, Stab Stitch

SPIDER MUM

Leaves: Sheer Ribbon Leaf

Stem: Chain Stitch, Couched Thread

Petals: Twisted Ribbon Stitch, Side Ribbon Stitch

*P*lease be aware that many different stitches could be used for one flower. I have given you suggestions and hope that you'll try some ideas of your own. Feel free to enlarge the sketches for personal use either by using the grids or by photocopy enlargement.

BULLION STITCH

Practice makes perfect with this stitch. Using a straw needle will help to make this wrapped stitch.

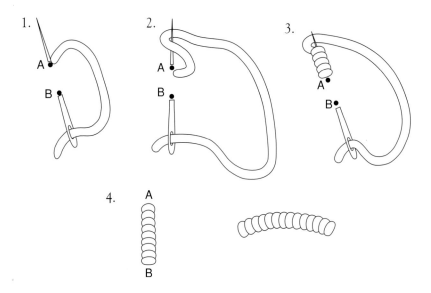

1. Decide the width of the stitch, then come up at A. Pull the thread through. Take the needle to the back at B. Come up again at A.

2. Raise the tip of the needle by holding it in your left hand and putting pressure on top of the needle eye. Wrap the needle clockwise

with the thread; pull the wrap firmly down toward the fabric.

3. Work the desired number of wraps until the wraps are the same width as the space from A to B. Pull the wraps firmly into place.

4. Hold the wraps and pull the needle through the wraps. Pull the thread through, holding firmly, and pull away from you in order to tighten the knot. Go back into point B to put the bullion in place.

BULLION, ROSEBUD

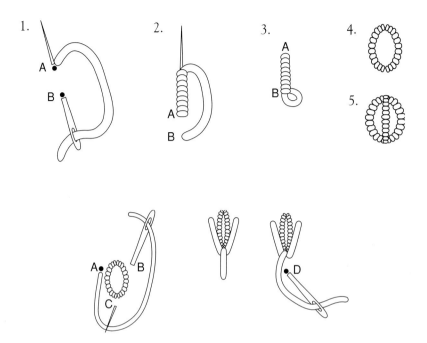

1. Come up at A; pull the thread through. Take the needle to the back at B. Come up again at A.

2. Wrap the needle clockwise for several wraps to fill the desired length. Hold the wraps firmly and pull the needle through, away from you.

3. Pull the wraps toward you and anchor the bullion by going back down at B.

4. If you are making two bullions, work the stitches so they curve toward each other.

5. If you are making three bullions, work the center bullion first, then add the right and left Bullion Stitches so they curve toward the center.

BUTTONHOLE, CIRCLE

A great stitch for hollyhocks and any saucer-shaped flower. I often use them for underwater fantasy shapes.

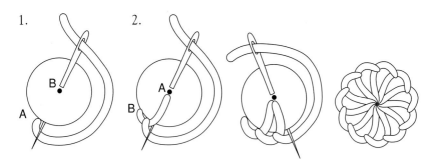

1. Draw a circle the desired size of the flower. Bring the needle up at the outside of the circle. You will be working counter-clockwise. Go down at center B and come up at the right of the thread at A. Make sure the needle is over the thread; pull firmly.

2. Continue around the circle until it is filled. Anchor in the back with a Slip Knot.

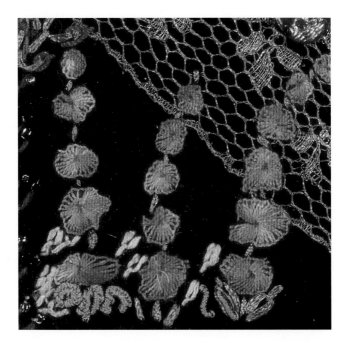

BUTTONHOLE, DETACHED

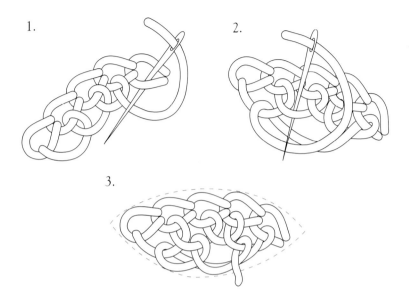

1. 2.

3.

1. Draw an outline of the leaf shape. Work a Chain Stitch along the top of the leaf. Work a row of Buttonhole Stitch loops from left to right. Keep the loops rather loose.

2. Once at the right side, take the thread back to the left. Start another set of loops.

3. Continue to the desired width, filling the designated shape.

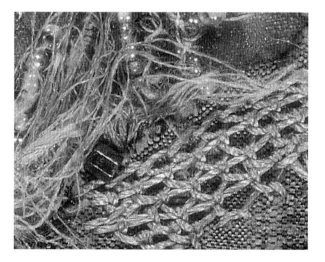

BUTTONHOLE, LOOP FLOWER

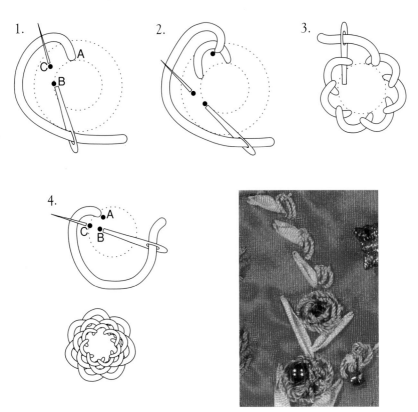

1. Draw two circles, one within the other. The outer circle is the actual size of the flower. Come up at A and go down at B, coming up at C (halfway between the two circles). Keep the needle over the thread.

2. Pull up, leaving the loop long enough to just touch the outer circle. Continue working around the circle until it is complete.

3. Repeat the same process in the inner circle. Come up just inside the inner circle, then continue working within the first circle of loops.

4. Continue working inner circles until the outer circle is filled. You may add French Knots to the center.

BUTTONHOLE SHAPES, TRIANGLE

Great stitch for foxgloves and hollyhocks. Work the start of the stitch as a Circle Buttonhole, but complete only one quarter of the circle. By working from small to big, you can give a floral effect.

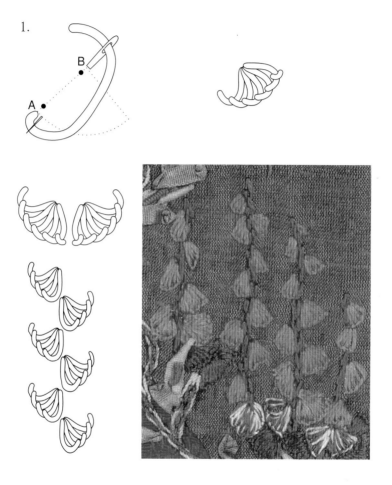

1. Draw the quarter circle shape. Come up at the outer left corner at A. Go back down at B, bringing the needle up close to A. Loop the thread under the needle; pull through. Work left to right.

CAST-ON STITCH FLOWER

The Cast-On Stitch is a Brazilian embroidery stitch which you can make into various flower shapes. Work each petal separately.

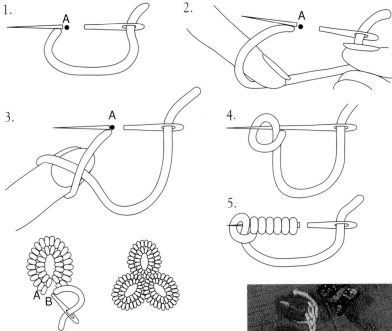

1. Come up at A. Take a small backstitch toward A and leave the needle in the fabric.

2. Grasp the thread in your right hand and lay it over your left index finger (which faces toward you).

3. Now twist your finger under the emerging thread so that the thread coming out of A lies on top.

4. Slip the loop onto the needle (cast-on). Pull the thread tight and slip the loop down toward the fabric.

5. Continue to cast on more loops until you have the desired length. Hold the cast-on and pull the needle and thread through the stitches.

CHAIN FLOWER, DETACHED

Good for trumpet shapes and flower shapes that need a continuous edge, such as daffodils, foxglove, and bellflowers.

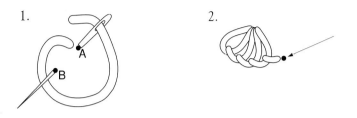

1. Come up at A. Go down at A again, as close as possible but not into it, and emerge at B. Make sure the needle lies over the loop; pull through.

2. Fill in the shape with the Buttonhole Stitch. Make the end by taking the thread just over the last loop.

CHINESE KNOT

Also called a Peking Knot, this stitch is often found in antique Chinese embroidery. Use as a filler stitch, and vary the colors of thread to achieve beautiful shading.

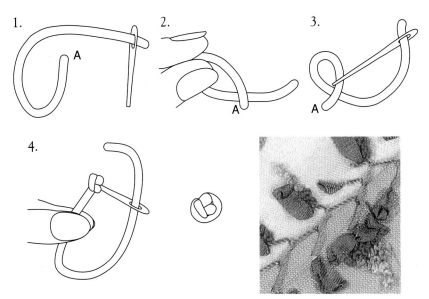

1. Come up at A. Loop the thread to the left.

2. Hold the loop down with your left thumb and finger. Pick up the loop and flip it over so the thread coming out of A is on the top.

3. Insert the needle inside the loop as close to A as possible, but not into it.

4. Pull the knot firmly into place. Holding the thread with your thumb, push the needle through to the back keeping the thread taut.

CHINESE KNOTTED LOOPS

Work the knot up to the point of pulling the thread through to the back of the fabric. Hold the loop at the desired length with the thumb; pull the thread through to the back. Tighten; the loop should sit on top of the knot.

CROCHET CHAIN STITCH

A free-form stitch that is wonderful texture for tree trunks; this stitch is worked with a crochet hook.

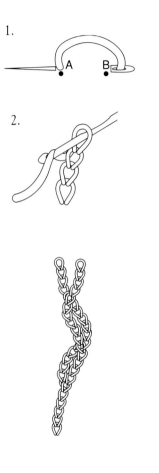

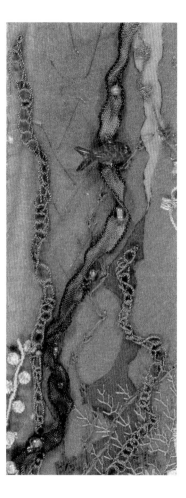

1. Make a small Straight Stitch: come up at A and go down at B. Come up at A again.

2. Remove the needle from the thread. With a crochet hook, reach under the Straight Stitch and work up a series of Chain Stitches. Work each to the desired length. Rethread the needle and anchor to the back. The Chain Stitch can be tacked down with another thread.

DRIZZLE STITCH FLOWER

A very effective Brazilian stitch. Use for underwater seaweeds and assorted flowers (best to use a straw needle).

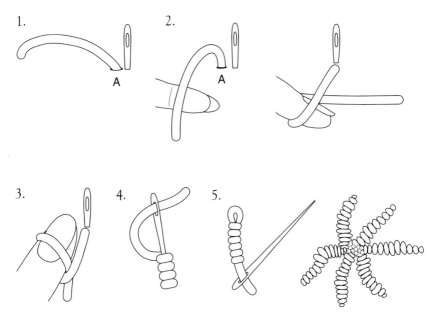

1. Come up at A. Unthread the needle and insert it next to A.

2. Place the thread over your left index finger. Rotate the finger towards you, holding the thread taut.

3. Slip the loop off your finger onto the needle. Pull the thread tight; slip the loop down the needle to the fabric. This is the first cast-on.

4. Work the desired number of Cast-on Stitches. Pull each stitch tightly and push them down onto the needle.

5. Rethread the needle. Pull the needle and thread through the Cast-on Stitches. This is the first petal, or drizzle. The stitches may be long or short.

END-STRING FLOWERS

Save bits and pieces of thread and ribbon to make these tufted flowers.

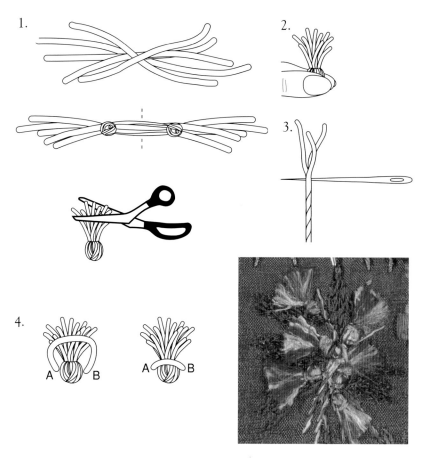

1. Take various lengths of thread and tie them in a series of Slip Knots, evenly spacing the knots.

2. Hold the pieces by the knot, and pull the ends up to form a loose pom-pom.

3. With a needle, separate any twisted threads to make the knots even fluffier.

4. Sew the shape in place, taking the needle through the ball and wrapping once around the pom-pom threads. Pull firmly in place.

Make plenty of these knotted flowers to keep for future projects.

ERMINE STITCH

Use as a textural stitch for filling in shapes. The stitch is named for its resemblance to crossed ermine tails.

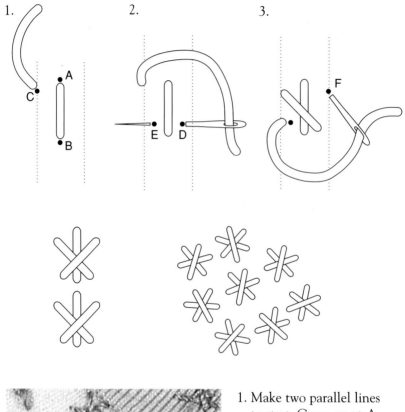

1. Make two parallel lines to start. Come up at A and go down at B. Exit at C.

2. Go back in at D, exiting at E.

3. Go back down at F to complete the stitch.

EYELET FLOWER

For flower shapes, Eyelet Stitches are all worked around the center hole. The Straight Stitches radiating out from the center hole can be free form or stitched in geometric shapes.

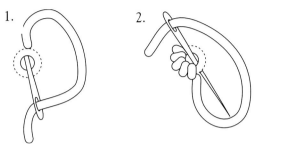

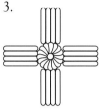

1. Gently pierce a hole in the fabric using an awl. Make a small Running Stitch just outside the hole. Take the needle through to the back.

2. Make an Overcast Stitch to cover the edge of the hole. Keep an even tension, and cover the Running Stitch. Finish the Overcast Stitch and take the thread to the back. End by running the thread under the stitches to secure.

3. Work four Straight Stitches on each side (or four Lazy Daisy Stitches), working from left to right.

Variation: FREE-FORM EYELETS

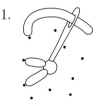

1. Gently pierce a hole with an awl into the fabric. Come up at an outside point. Go down into the center hole and come up again.

2. Work the Straight Stitches around the center hole. Pull firmly to keep the hole open.

FEATHER STITCH LEAF

A free-form leaf that is easy to do because the stitiches can be uneven.

1.   2.

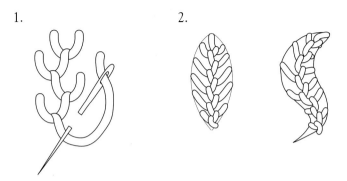

1. Draw an outline of a leaf shape. Start at the top of the leaf with the first stitch. Alternate the stitches left and right, working them downward in a vertical column.

2. Work out to the outside lines. These stitches are uneven and meant to be free-form. Can also be worked in multiple layers of color.

FISHBONE STITCH

A great stitch to make ferns and leaves.

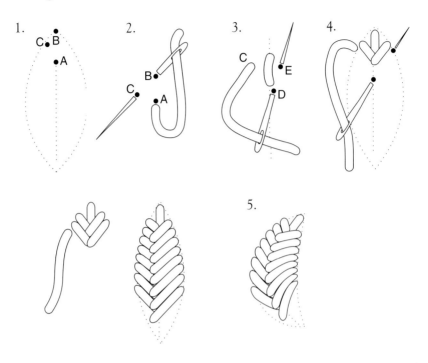

1. Draw an outline of the leaf. Come up at A on the center line. Go down at B and back up at C.

2. Keep the thread on the right side of the needle.

3. Pull the thread through. Now with the thread on the left, go from D to E.

4. Continue stitching to form the shape.

5. When working on a curve, tighten up the stitches on the inside of the curve. Space apart the stitches on the outer portion of the curve.

FLY STITCH, CIRCLE

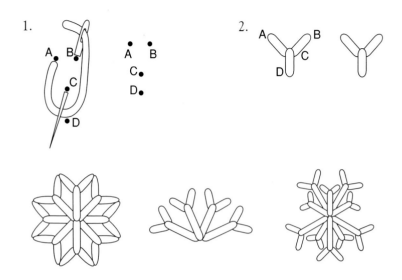

1. Come up at A; pull the thread through. Make a loop: go down at B and come up at C, over the thread; pull in place.

2. Go down at D to finish off. The Fly Stitch looks like the letter Y. Use the Fly Stitch to form texture or whimsical flower shapes (or even snowflakes).

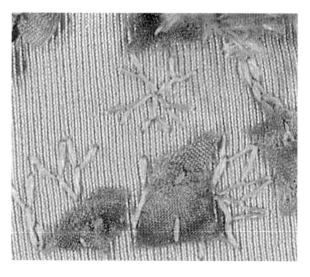

FLY STITCH, DANDELION SEED POD

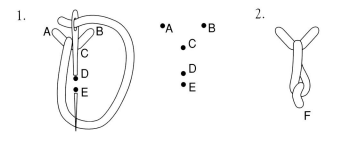

1. Work up a Fly Stitch from points A to C.

2. Hold the thread over to the left side. Make a small Lazy Daisy Stitch: Go down at D and up at E. Pull into place, making sure the needle lies over the thread. Anchor with a Catch Stitch at F.

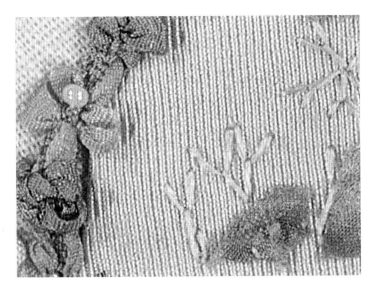

FLY STITCH LEAF

A soft-looking pretty leaf which can curl to the left or right. Keep the Fly Stitches an irregular length.

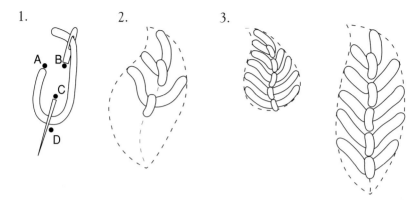

1. Draw an outline of the leaf shape. Make a Fly Stitch: Come up at A, go down at B, emerging at C. Go down at D.

2. Work a series of free-form Fly Stitches, going to the outside edges of the leaf. The center, or spine, of the leaf will be where the Catch Stitch (D) of the Fly Stitch is placed.

3. For variation, use with two or three shades of green thread, working from dark to light. Come in with a second shade of green. Work a series of Fly Stitches between the previous Fly Stitches.

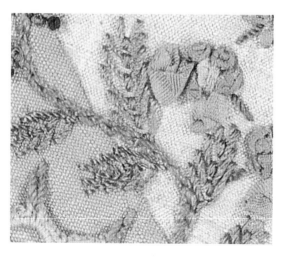

GRANITOS

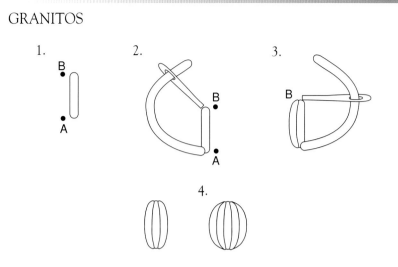

1. Come up at A and go down at B.

2. Come back up at A in the same hole. Pull the thread through. Loop the thread to the left and go back down at B (through the same hole); pull through and position the thread on the left.

3. Come back up at A and loop the thread to the right. Go back down at B.

4. Add extra stitches to make a larger Granito. The small bud-like shape may look different based on the number of stitches.

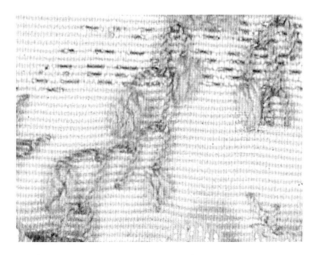

LAZY DAISY BULLION KNOT

1.

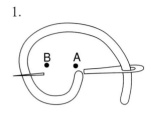

2.

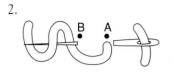

3.

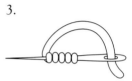

4.

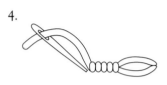

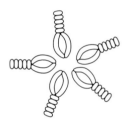

1. Bring the thread up at A. Form a loop. Go back in at A and come out at B. Pull the loop snugly under the needle.

2. Take the thread going into the needle and wrap the thread clockwise around the needle tip.

3. Make four or five wraps. Pull the wraps snugly.

4. Hold the wraps firmly with the left thumb. Pull the thread through the wraps. Pull the wraps snugly. Anchor the stitch. Use the tip of the needle to push the wraps in place.

LAZY DAISY, DOUBLE

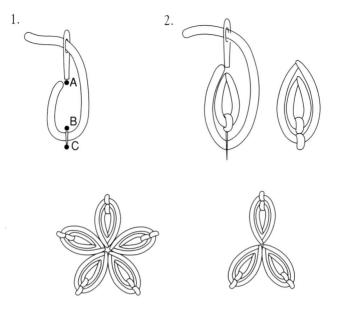

1. Come up at A and form a loop. Bring the thread to the top side. Go back down at A and come up at B. Make sure the needle lies over the thread; pull through.

2. Go down at C, forming a Catch Stitch. Come up just above A, forming a larger Lazy Daisy on the outside.

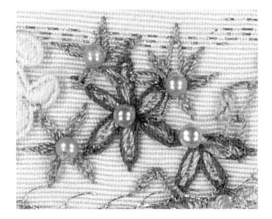

NEEDLEWEAVING BAR

This stitch is used in needle lace, but makes good leaves, petals, and sepals. Each bar is woven above the fabric with only the tip attached.

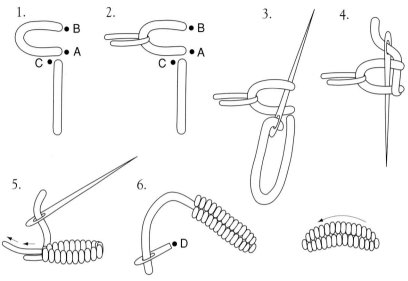

1. Come up at A. Form a loop and go down at B. Decide how wide the bar should be. Come up just below A at C.

2. Pass a piece of thread through the loop (I use a bobby pin or a paper clip). Hold the loop off the fabric.

3. Weave over the bottom thread and under the top. Reverse the needle.

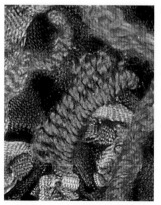

4. Come back over the top thread and under the bottom. Each time, push the woven thread snugly down to the previous wraps.

5. Once the loop is completely wrapped, pull the holding thread.

6. To make the bar curve, go into the fabric at D (just a bit shorter than the length of the bar for the curve).

NET STITCH

A wonderful stitch for seaweed and fantasy leaves.

1.

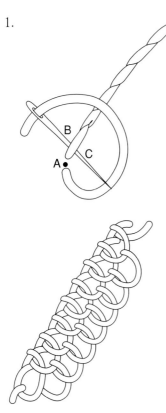

2.

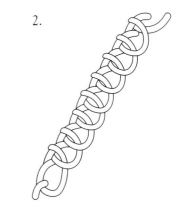

1. Make a row of Outline Stitches to act as an anchor for the first row of loose Buttonhole Stitches. Using a new thread, come up on the left end of the Outline Stitch row. Holding the thread down, slide the needle under the first Outline Stitch, forming a loose Buttonhole Stitch. Make sure the needle lies over the loop.

2. Repeat this process for each row.

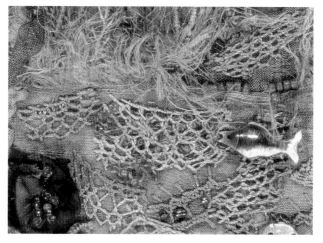

OYSTER STITCH

This stitch is a combination of Twisted Chain Stitches, a good stitch to use for texture and single petal shapes.

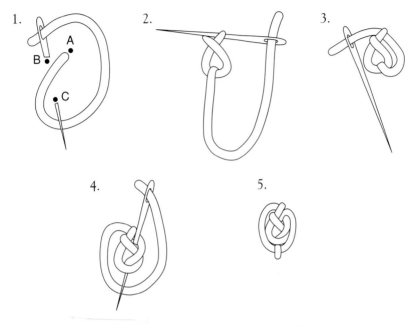

1. Come up at A and form a loop. Go back at B and come up at C with the needle over the thread. Pull the stitch into place.

2. Slide the needle under the right-hand thread, just below A.

3. Pull the thread through and allow the thread to lie on the right side of the twisted chain.

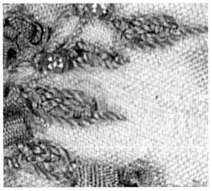

4. Go to the back, to the right of the twist and inside the loop. Come up at the base with the needle over the loop.

5. Pull the thread through; the second loop lies around the first loop. Anchor the loop by taking a Catch Stitch.

PORTUGUESE KNOTTED STEM

A good outline stitch also used for making stems and branches (similar to a String of Pearls, but has a fuller look).

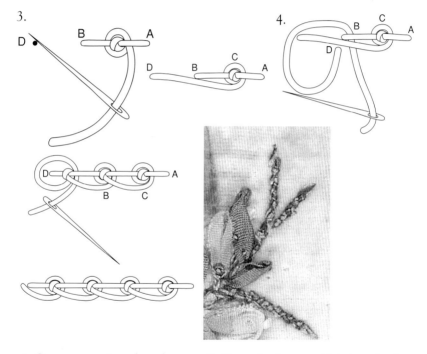

1. Come up at A and go down at B. Come back up at C, below the bar. Wrap the thread up and over the bar. Come down under the bar on the right side of C. Pull gently in place.

2. Wrap around a second time, bringing the needle under the bar between the knot and A. Pull gently into place.

3. Insert the needle at point D. Come back up at B, below the bar, for the second knot.

4. Repeat the same process to finish the desired length.

RAISED STRAIGHT STITCH

1.

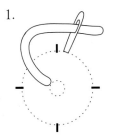

2.

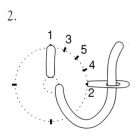

1. Mark the outer circle shape with dots. Mark a second smaller circle in the center. Divide the circle into quarters as shown.

2. Work each quarter circle with Straight Stitches until the circle is complete. Fill the center with French Knots. Raise the Straight Stitches by running the needle under the stitches and gently pulling up.

SPIDERWEB, BACKSTITCH

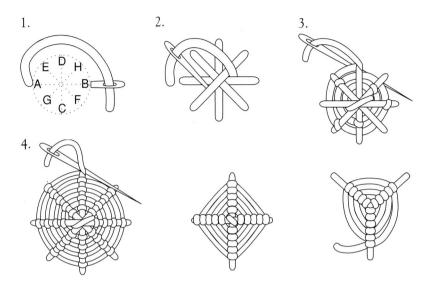

1. Using a tapestry needle, stitch the spokes as shown, pulling each spoke firmly in place.

2. Take a small Catch Stitch in the center, holding down all the spokes.

3. Come up to the top in the center. Slide under one spoke.

4. Continue working, easing back over one spoke and advancing under two. Continue until the spokes are filled; wrap the thread back around the spoke.

STRING OF PEARLS

This stitch can be worked with the knots spaced closely to form a beaded edge, or apart to look like seaweed or a branch.

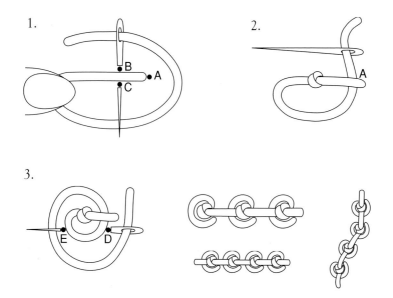

1. Come up at A. Hold the thread in a horizontal line with the left hand. Hold the needle perpendicular to the thread and take a small stitch down at B. Come up at C. The needle lies over the thread; pull firmly into place.

2. Take the thread up under the bar to the right of the knot. Lay the thread in a small circle that surrounds the knot.

3. Go down just below the bar at D, close to the knot. Come up to the left of the knot at E; pull firmly. Continue stitching to make knots to the desired length of the stitch.

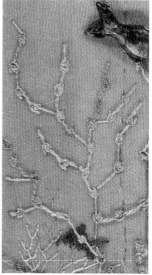

TUFTED FLOWER

A very free-form stitch to use for thistle and fuzzy-looking flowers.

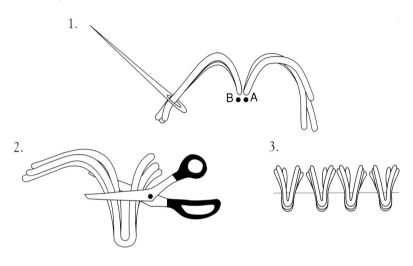

1.

B • • A

2.

3.

1. Thread up with three or four strands of thread. Do not pull the thread into a knot. Go down at A and come up as close as possible to A (at B). Decide how long the tufts will be.

2. With sharp scissors, clip the threads to the desired length.

3. The tufts will stay in place. Work the tufts close together to fill in the desired area.

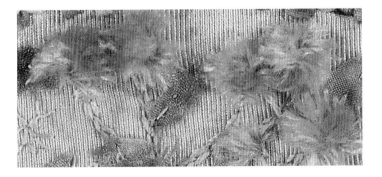

VANDYKE STITCH

A good stitch for wheat or barley shapes. This stitch should be worked upside down so the "V" flares up at the top.

1.

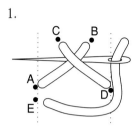

2.

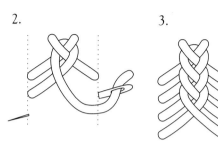

3.

1. Work this stitch between two parallel lines. Come up at A, go down at B, and emerge at C. Go down at D and emerge at E.

2. Slide the needle under the crossed threads and gently pull the loop in place.

3. The V (shape) formed at the top of the stitch will flare out.

VICTORIAN POM-POMS

Very textured free-form pom-pom to use for 3-dimensional flowers, such as chrysanthemums and Lilies of the Nile.

1.

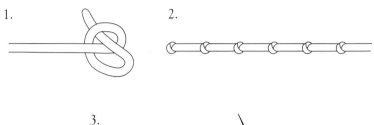

2.

3.

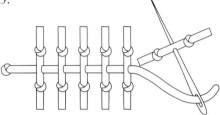

1. Use about 18" of thread. Make twenty evenly spaced Loop Knots.

2. Cut the thread as shown. (This section is one bead unit.)

3. With a fine needle and thread, pierce the center thread of the bead unit. Gather the beads by weaving the thread under the units to join. Trim the ends and gather the beads to make one pom-pom.

WHEAT EAR, DETACHED

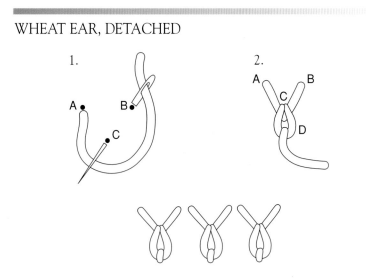

1. Come up at A. Go down at B and back out at C. Keep the needle over the looped thread. Pull down and hold the thread with your free hand.

2. Make a second loop. Go down at C and up at D. Anchor the stitch (similar to a Lazy Daisy) with a small Straight Stitch.

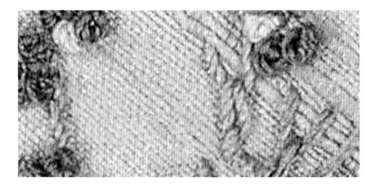

WOOL ROSE

Use tapestry yarn for this easy, effective rose.

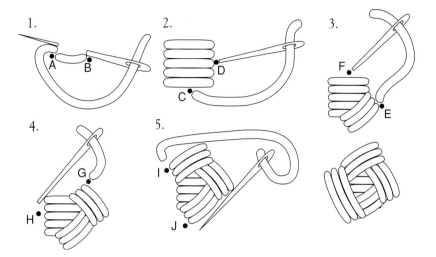

1. Come up at A and back in at B. Bring the needle up a few threads above A. Pull the wool through to make the first stitch. Continue in the same way to make a total of five stitches, making a square center.

2. With a lighter shade of yarn, bring the thread up at the center of the bottom side of the square (C). Go down at the center of the right side (D). Bring the thread up just to the right of C and take it to the back a bit higher and wider than D. Repeat to make a total of three stitches.

3. Bring the wool up at E (overlapping D) and go down at F. Come up just to the right of E and take it to the back a bit higher and wider than F. Repeat to make a total of three stitches.

4. Bring the wool up at G (overlapping F) and go down at H, following the same method as previous steps to make a total of three stitches.

5. Bring the thread up at I (overlapping H) and go down at J, just to the right and a bit lower than C (overlapping C). Repeat the process to make a total of three stitches to form four petals.

WOOL ROSEBUD

1.   2.   3.   4.   5.

B
A

C

D

F
E

1. Come up at A and down at B.

2. Alternating left to right, work four more stitches. Keep the stitches flat by running the needle under them each time.

3. Work the outer petals in a different shade. Come up left of the base center and take the wool thread up about two-thirds to the right side. Work two more stitches to complete the first petal.

4. Change to a third shade of wool. Come up to the right of the base, overlapping the first petal. Take the wool up two-thirds of the bud. Work three stitches to complete the bud.

5. Change to green thread for the sepal. Make two short Straight Stitches at the base. Work the stem with the same green as the sepal. Use an Outline Stitch or a Whip Stitch.

WOVEN PICOT

Use for a leaf or a petal.

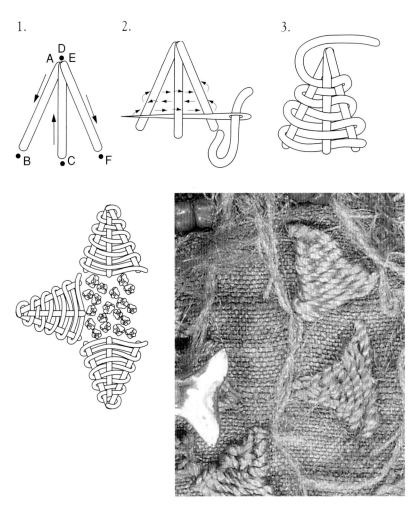

1. Using a tapestry needle, work a pyramid of three Straight Stitches the desired length of the petal. Make a secure knot at the back to secure the anchor stitch.

2. Come up at the bottom of the right anchor stitch.

3. Weave under and over until you come to the tip. Go to the back and make a secure knot.

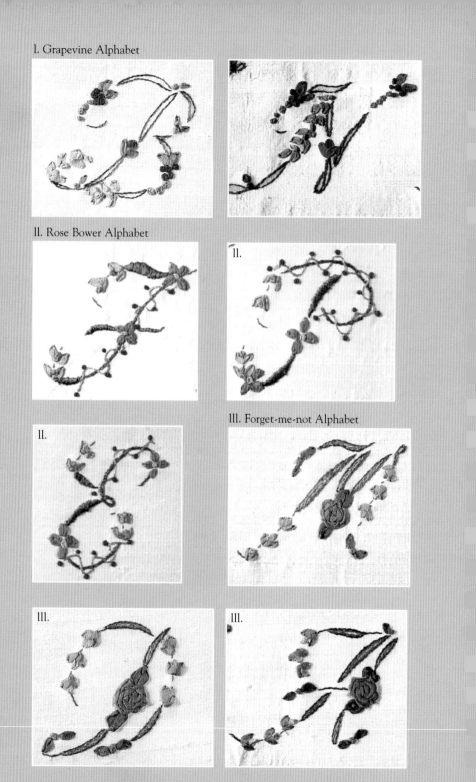

l. Grapevine Alphabet

ll. Rose Bower Alphabet

ll.

ll.

lll. Forget-me-not Alphabet

lll.

lll.

ALPHABETS AND MONOGRAMS

Everyone enjoys seeing their name written out. Now you can use these beautiful alphabets to monogram clothing and linens. The floral area of the alphabet is interchangeable by using the three patterns presented. Enlarge the letters or make them smaller with a copy machine, taking care to not distort the letters.

1. Grapevine Alphabet

1. Grapevine Alphabet

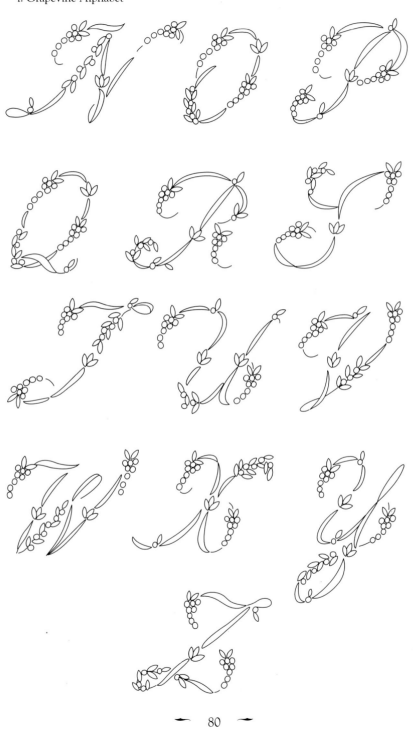

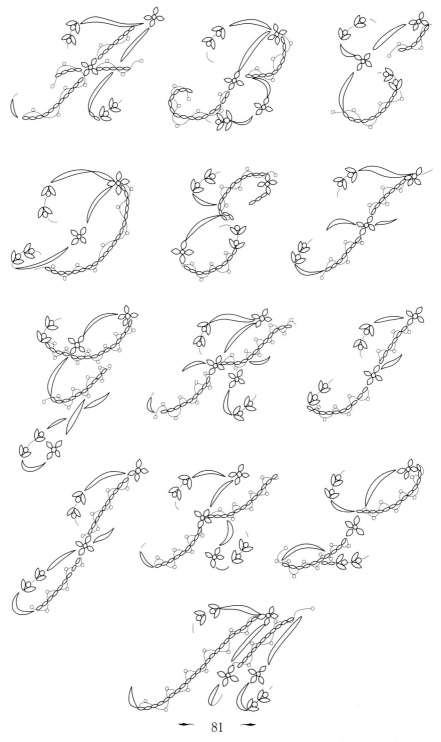

11. Forget-me-not Alphabet

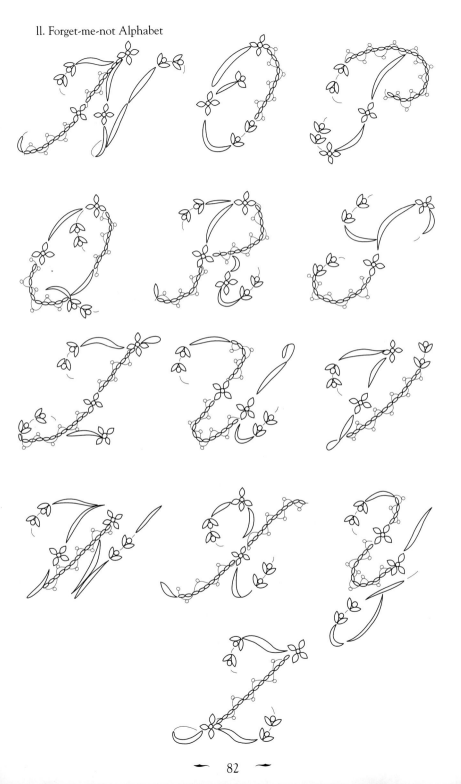

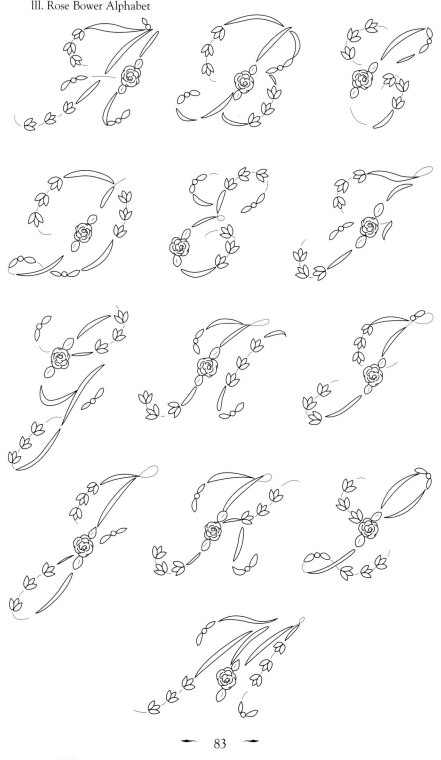

lll. Rose Bower Alphabet

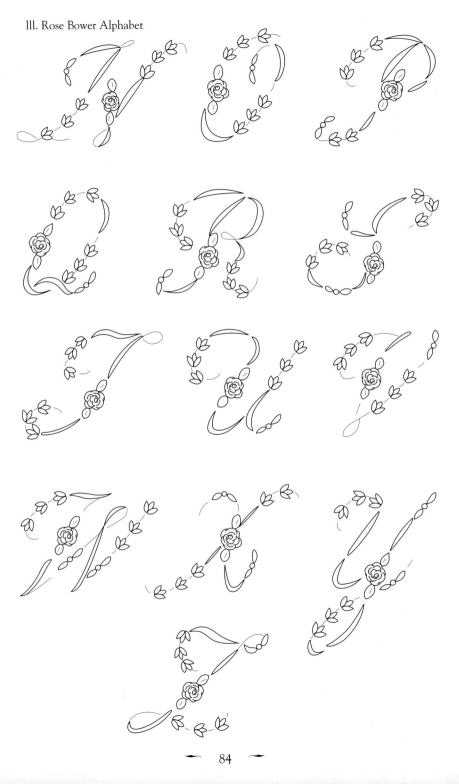

RIBBON EMBROIDERY STITCHES

CHRISTINE'S BLOSSOMS

A lovely little blossom taught to me by my friend Christine Simpson of Scarlet Ribbons, Perth, Australia. They are a bit fiddley, but well worth the effort.

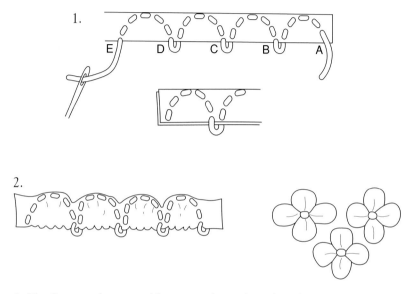

1. Use 3mm-wide satin ribbon, matching thread, and a fine needle. Work right to left. Start running stitches at A and create ½" wide arches. Make sure the thread loops over the edges at points B, C, and D.

2. Finish at point E and gently gather at this point. Four little petals will form. Join the edges and sew in place.

FOLDED RIBBON ROSE

Can be made from various widths and types of ribbon. The size of the rose is decided by the width of the ribbon and the number of folds.

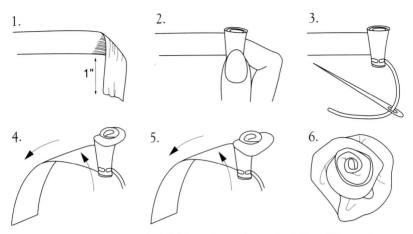

1. Make a 90-degree angled fold on the right end of the ribbon, about 1" from the end.

2. Roll firmly in a clockwise direction for three turns, to form the center of the rose.

3. Stitch firmly at the lower edge of the roll, through all the layers of ribbon. Let the needle and thread dangle.

4. With the left thumb and forefinger, fold the top edge of the ribbon back and down (fold lies on top of the twist).

5. Wrap around the center to form the first petal. Pick up the dangling needle and anchor the folded petal, piercing all layers of ribbon. Pull tight; make a Slip Knot. Let the needle dangle.

6. Begin the second petal, using the left thumb and forefinger. Fold the top edge back and down as before, secure as before. Continue around, securing each petal; continue folding, wrapping, and stitching until the rose is the desired size (three or four more rounds). Clip the ends and sew in place.

FOLDED ROSEBUD

The folded rosebud is simply a rolled center and one petal of the folded rose.

1.

2.

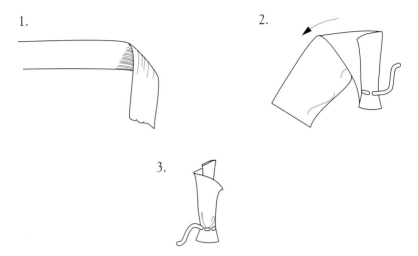

3.

1. Make a 90-degree angle 1" from the right end. Make three tight rolls from right to left. Anchor tightly at the base.

2. Make a petal by folding back and down. Wrap this petal counter-clockwise, angling the petal toward the base of the bud.

3. Anchor at the base and secure.

FRENCH KNOT FLOWER

A small, loose, loopy stitch which can be used separately or in a cluster.

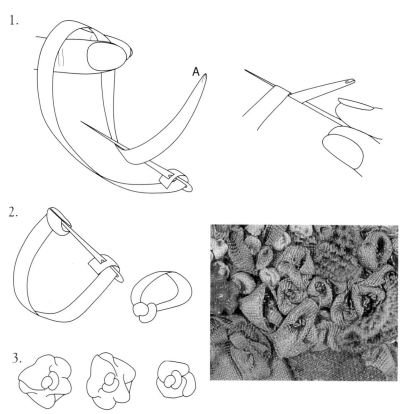

1. Use a short length of ribbon (12"). Come up at A. Make one full wrap on the needle.

2. Go back into the fabric as close to A as possible. Do not pull the knot tight. Pull the needle and ribbon gently to the back. Leave a very loose French Knot on the fabric.

3. With thread, come up in the center of the ribbon knot and make a French Knot to anchor the ribbon (forms the center of the flower). Some people prefer to let the ribbon hang in the back while they thread up, and sew a French Knot with thread in the center of the ribbon. I prefer to make up several ribbon French Knots and then come back to anchor them with thread French Knots.

GATHERED RIBBON FLOWER

A big, full flower that could be a rose, peony, or chrysanthemum. Make with silk or organza ribbon. The size of the flower is determined by the length of the ribbon. Change the look of the flower by using variegated or ombre ribbon, or by using two different widths together.

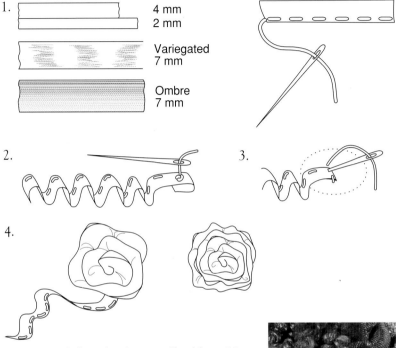

1. Cut a 15" length of 7mm silk ribbon. Using Nymo™ thread or a matching color thread, sew a line of small running stitches along the edge of the ribbon.

2. Pull up the running stitches until the length is halved. Even out gathers. Fold the end down and secure with a Slip Knot.

3. Draw the shape of the flower onto the fabric. Now, anchor the ribbon to the center of the flower shape using two small stitches through the edge of the ribbon.

4. Fold the ribbon around the center. Stitch it in place every ⅛" or so. Continue around in a spiral, until the shape is filled. End by turning the ribbon edge under and attach it with two small stitches. Go to the back and make a Slip Knot.

HELEN'S ANTIQUE ROSE

Helen Eriksson is a household name in Australia. Her silk ribbon florals are breathtaking and often appear in needlework magazines. She is the author of a *Ribbon Renaissance: Artistry in Silk*.

1. Use the Japanese Ribbon Stitch and 4mm-wide ribbon for small roses or 7mm-wide ribbon for larger roses. For base petals, start from the center using the darkest shade. The petals will curve upward.

2. Add the shadow petals using a lighter shade.

3. Add four outer bowl petals, keeping them loose. Add a few more petals inside the outer bowl petals.

4. Work French Knots to fill in the center. Add three or four shorter petals in the center front. Add a couple of base petals if necessary.

IRIS STITCH

Quick and easy and oh, so effective! The Iris Stitch is a combination of the Lazy Daisy, Loop Stitch, and Colonial Knot.

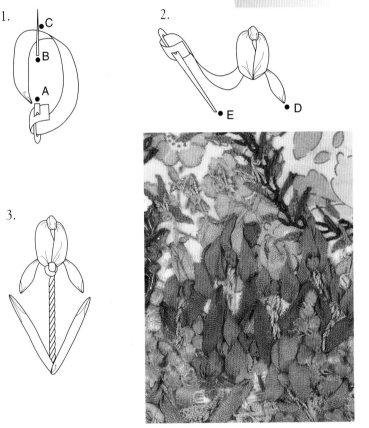

1. Form a loose Lazy Daisy: Come up at A, then form a loop going back down at A and up at B. Pull one loop gently into place. Anchor the loop at C.

2. Come up at D and slide the ribbon under the base of the Lazy Daisy (try to keep it smooth). Go down at E leaving the ribbon base at the curve.

3. Make a Colonial Knot at the base of the Lazy Daisy. Add a stem and long Japanese Ribbon Stitches for leaves.

JAN'S ANTIQUE ROSE

Jan Bond of Adelaide, Australia, is an expert embroiderer and a friend to me and my family cat Sam! Her work is featured in major Australian needlework magazines. Her antique roses are beautiful.

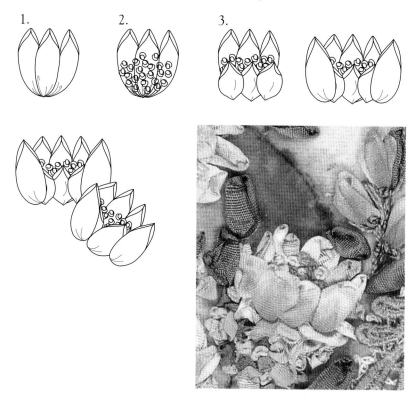

1. Use 4mm ribbon for small roses or 7mm ribbon for medium roses. Stitch three Japanese Ribbon Stitches close together.

2. With thread, fill in with French Knots. These will show toward the top and will act as padding for the overlapping stitches.

3. Add five Japanese Ribbon Stitches. Work the front three ribbon stitches, keeping them very loose. Use the needle to slide under each stitch and gently pull to give it more fullness. Add two longer ribbon stitches on either side. Roses can be made much larger and looser by adding more petals and varying the shades of color.

JAPANESE WIRE RIBBON BUD

An unusual bud that looks beautiful tucked into silk-ribbon embroidery.

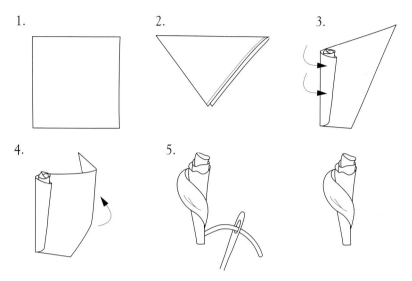

1. Use a wide, wire-edged ombre ribbon. Cut a piece the exact length of the width of the ribbon to form a square.

2. Fold the piece into a triangle, with the fold on top.

3. Fold one wing tightly into the center (to look like a sausage).

4. Fold the other wing backward and down, keeping it rather loose, to form a bud or lily shape.

5. Using a strong thread, pierce the bottom and wrap tightly. Make a Slip Stitch. Cut the excess ribbon and sew the bud in place.

JOYCE FLOWER (FARGO FLOWER)

Sometimes a mistake can result in a most wonderful flower. While at the Fargo, N.D. Quilt Conference, Joyce Valley was trying to do Ruched Ribbon Rosettes, and this is the result. It makes wonderful marigolds; and, when worked in a cluster, acacia blossoms (called "wattle" in Australia). Size can vary depending on the number of running stitches.

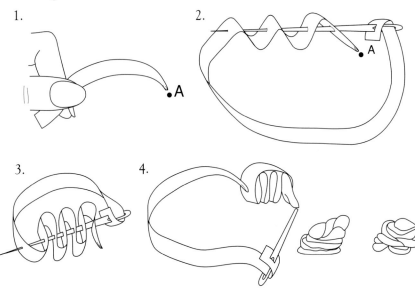

1. Use about 12" of 4mm-wide silk ribbon and a chenille needle. Come up at A and hold the ribbon in your free hand.

2. With the tip of the needle held very close to point A, take three to five long running stitches.

3. Now, gently pull the needle through the running stitches.

4. Go back down as close to point A as possible. Pull the ribbon through and pull gently into place. This is a free-form gathered flower, very useful as a filler or individual flower.

JUDITH'S CURLED LEAF

A lovely stitch for tiny-to-medium length leaves, it can be worked in 4mm, 7mm, and 12mm silk ribbon. This is a variation on the Japanese Ribbon Stitch.

1.

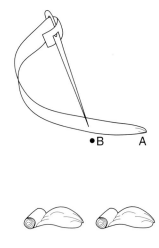

2.

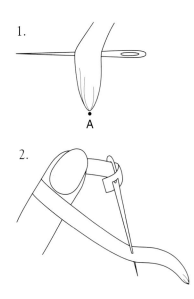

1. Come up at A. Slide the needle under the ribbon to smooth it out. Decide on the length of the stitch, and with the tip of the needle at B, push the ribbon (in the center) into a curl or curve.

2. Pierce through to the fabric below and gently pull the ribbon through. Use your finger or a laying tool to keep it smooth and even. Do not let the ribbon twist.

JUDITH'S KNOTTED FLOWERS

Use my quick and easy method to make knotted shaggy flowers.

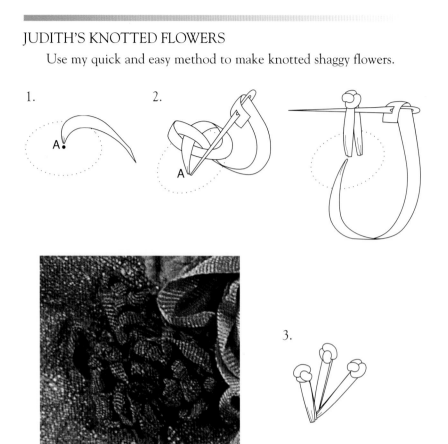

1. Draw the outline of the flower on the fabric using a water-erasable pen. Use 4mm silk ribbon (about 12") in three different shades, and a chenille needle. Come up at A with the ribbon.

2. Make a Slip Knot at the desired height (¼" to ½"). With the needle tip, work the knot into place. Tighten the knot. Come up again near A, and use the needle as a laying tool to make sure both sides of the knot are even. Go back down as close to A as possible.

3. Repeat the process until the area is filled.

ELLY'S WIRE RIBBON PANSY

Elly Sienkiewicz, author of many best-selling books including *Romancing Ribbons into Flowers*, is a multi-talented artist and a dear friend. She is sharing with us her Wire Ribbon Pansy.

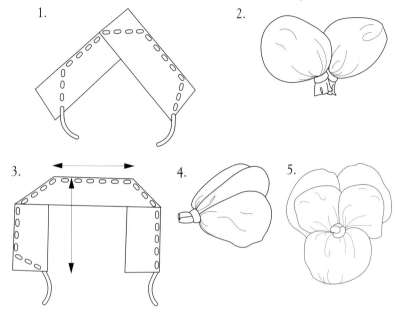

1. Cut a length of ribbon for the back petal. Fold the ribbon in half at a 90° angle. Add a running stitch along the ribbon edge.

2. Gather the ribbon to form a petal. Repeat the process for a second back petal.

3. For the front petals, cut one length of ribbon and fold into three equal sections. Add a running stitch along the ribbon edge.

4. Gather the ribbon to form the three front petals. Wrap the thread around the ribbon ends to secure the center.

5. Unfold the ribbon to form the three petals. Secure the two back petals to the front three-petal unit. Add a bead for the center or use ribbon or embroidery thread to cover the pansy center.

LAZY DAISY ROSEBUD

A simple but effective rosebud that combines a Lazy Daisy, Fly Stitch, and Colonial Knot.

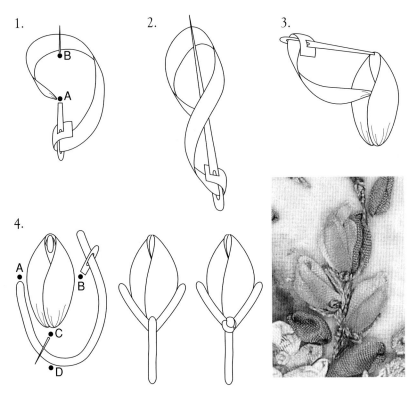

1. Start to make a Lazy Daisy with silk ribbon. Come up at A. Form a loop. Go back down in A and up at B.

2. As you tighten the loop, keep it as flat and smooth as possible. Working the ribbon gently into place, pull the ribbon through point B.

3. Now, pierce the ribbon at the top of the loop. Pull into place to secure the stitch. Let the Catch Stitch remain a bit loose; don't pull too tight.

4. With thread or yarn, make a Fly Stitch. (Come up at A, go down at B, and emerge at C. Go down at D to make the Catch Stitch.) Add a Colonial Knot at the base to form the calyx.

LAZY DAISY WITH FRENCH KNOT

A Lazy Daisy Stitch that is held in place with a French Knot. Makes wonderful buds and free-form flowers.

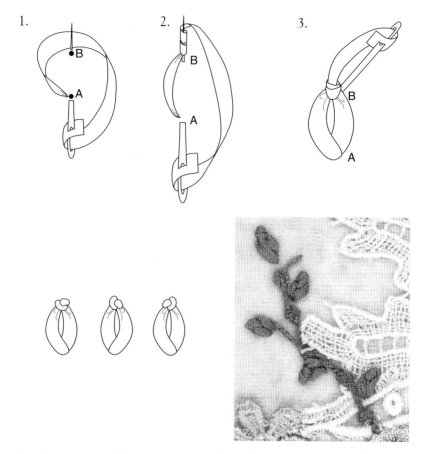

1. Using a 4mm ribbon, come up at A, go back down in A and come up again at B. Pull the ribbon loop snugly down around the needle. With the tip extending beyond the ribbon (just so the eye of the needle remains) raise the needle tip. Apply pressure to the eye of the needle. Make sure the needle lies over the loop of ribbon.

2. Wrap clockwise around the needle. Make two wraps. Hold the wraps with the left thumb and pull the ribbon through the wraps.

3. Pull firmly and go back down as close to point B as possible. Catch the ribbon loop as you go down with the needle.

LOOP STITCH

A wonderful filler stitch and great for making flowers such as hydrangeas. The loops are perfect for greenery and interspersed throughout delphiniums, snapdragons, and lupines.

1.

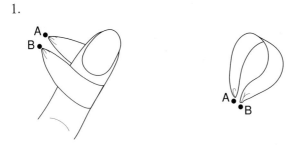

1. Using 4mm silk ribbon, come up at A and go back down at B. When pulling the ribbon through, keep it smooth and flat. Use your finger or a laying tool to prevent it from twisting. Gently pull it to the desired length.

2. Work the loops close together. (Please use caution, as this stitch can be pulled out if you pull too hard.)

LOOP FLOWER

This is a handy stitch that can be worked in various widths of silk ribbon. Good to use as florets of lantana, waxflower, delphinium, and hydrangea.

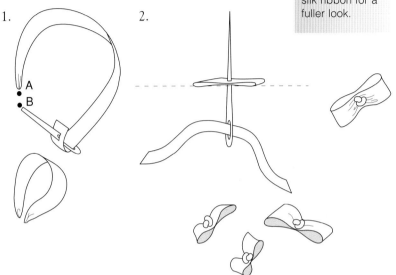

1. Come up at A and go down at B. Pull the ribbon gently to the back. Do not let the ribbon twist. Use a laying tool or your finger to keep the loop straight. Pull the loop down to the desired size.

2. Thread a needle with the desired thread. Flatten the ribbon loop, so the loops are even. Bring the thread up into the center of the loop. Make a French Knot. Pull tightly so the two sides of the ribbon form a bow.

MOKUBA FLOWER

Mr. Watanabe, owner of Mokuba Ribbons, has been very good to me. He is also very creative and showed me how to make this little flower with a flame and 1½" of ribbon. You must use Mokuba picot-edge polyester ombre ribbon. It comes in six different color variations which go from light to dark.

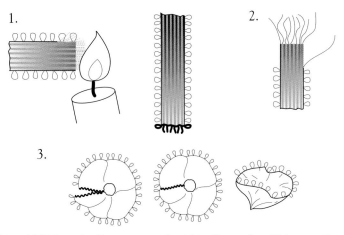

1. Cut a 1½" length. Burn one end with a flame. It will have a hard melted edge.

2. Unravel the unburned horizontal thread until a fringe is showing.

3. Decide if the flower will have a light or dark center. Holding the ribbon loosely in your free hand, pull the outside vertical thread of the dark or light side until that side is gathered tightly. Holding the

gathered side in place, burn the raw edge as in Step 1 to melt the threads. This will hold the gathered edge in place. Let one end overlap the other to form a small cupped flower. With matching thread, sew it in place. Make sure to leave the outer edges free. Fill in center with beads or French Knots.

PANSY STITCH

This cheerful little pansy is quick and easy. Select three shades of 4mm silk ribbon, one being the base shade, such as purple. (Can be worked in wide ribbon.)

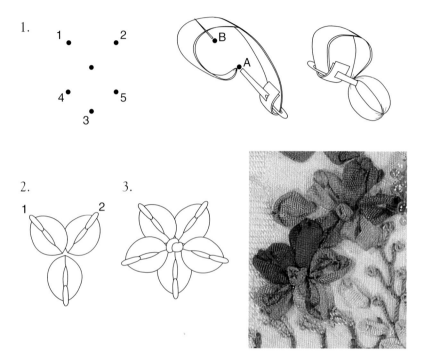

1. Mark the center of the pansy with a dot on the fabric. Add five additional dots, as shown. Thread a chenille needle with the base shade and one of the three shades. Treat it as one ribbon. The first (or base) shade goes on top. Come up in the center mark and work a loose Lazy Daisy. Work a second Lazy Daisy (2).

2. Using the base shade and the second shade, work next petal (3). The second shade goes on top.

3. Using the third and base shade, work the remainng (4 & 5) petals. The third shade goes on top. Work a Colonial Knot in the center. Using a dark thread, work a Straight Stitch in the center of the three bottom petals.

FIVE-PETAL GATHERED FLOWER

The size of this five-sided flower will vary depending on the width of the ribbon and the width of the five intervals.

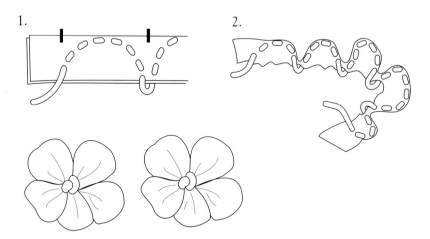

1. For ⅝" wide ribbon, cut a length 7⅜" long. Mark at 1⅜" intervals. Using a running stitch, make five half-circles. Make sure to loop under the ribbon edge at the bottom of each half-curve. This ensures that the thread will gather up easily.

2. Gently pull the running-stitch thread, gathering the ribbon into five petals. When the petals are pulled into place, sew the two ends together and trim away any excess. Add French Knots or Pistil Stitches to the center.

RIBBON SPLIT STITCH

This is a wonderful stitch for branches, limbs, seaweed, and different grasses. The Split Stitch is worked the same way if using yarn or thread.

TIP
If worked with fine thread, this stitch is known as the Kensington Outline Stitch, and can be used to outline or to act as a filler. Shading can be achieved with this stitch if it is worked in rows.

1.

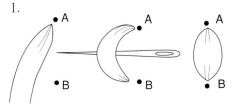

2.   3.

1. Come up at A and go down at B. Use the needle to keep the ribbon flat.

2. Come up in the center of the Straight Stitch at point C, flatten the ribbon with the needle, and go back down at D.

3. Continue stitching for the desired length.

RAISED RIBBON STITCH

A lovely open multi-petaled flower. Using fewer petals, it can be made into other flowers. Use 4mm silk or organza ribbon (ribbon up to 12mm will also work).

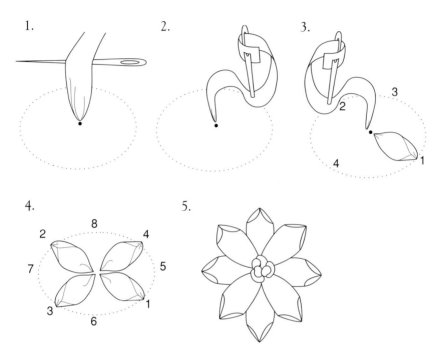

1. 2. 3.

4. 5.

1. Draw a circle which will be the actual size of the flower. Draw a dot in the center. Come up just above the center dot with the ribbon. Use the needle to flatten the ribbon.

2. Gently raise the ribbon to form a curve, and pierce the ribbon at the drawn-circle line (in the center of the ribbon).

3. Carefully pull the ribbon through, until the end starts to curl and pops through. Come up directly below the dot and put in the second petal.

4. Add petals three and four to make a cross. Add petals five, six, seven, and eight to make a full flower.

5. Add French Knots to the center.

RIBBON STITCH PANSY

This loose, blowsy pansy is a variation of the Raised Ribbon Stitch and can be worked with a wider ribbon.

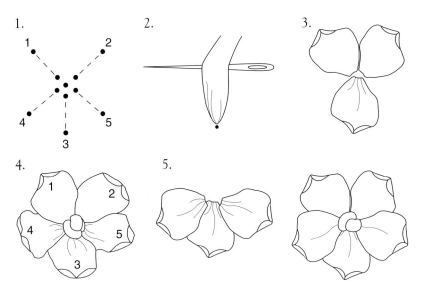

1. Mark dots as shown. Come up just beyond the center mark.

2. Gently slide the needle under the ribbon to flatten the ribbon, then gently lift it up. Pierce the ribbon in the center at the marked dot. Pull the ribbon through until it curls (making a Japanese Ribbon Stitch) and pops through, leaving two curled lips.

3. Work the next petal (2) until they are snug against the first. Change the color of ribbon and work the bottom petal (3) in the same way. Use your needle to spread the ribbon.

4. Using a third shade of ribbon, make the final two stitches. Fill the center with a Colonial Knot, keeping it rather loose.

5. Using a dark thread, put in three fan-shaped Straight Stitches on each of the three bottom petals.

RUTH'S ROSETTES

Ruth Stonely of Brisbane, Australia, is a wonderful designer and a dear friend. She taught me how to make this sweet little floral stitch that is heavenly on lingerie or baby clothes. Use it as a meandering stitch or to fill crazy quilt seams. Can also zigzag or form geometric patterns.

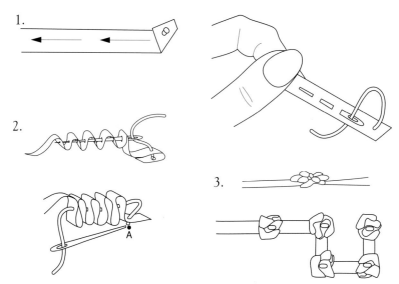

1. Take a length of 4mm silk ribbon. Using a metallic, smooth thread on a fine needle, anchor an end of the ribbon firmly into the edge of the fabric. Go to the back of the fabric. Keep a space between each rosette, usually ¼" to ⅛". Come up ¼" beyond the anchor stitches. Hold the ribbon in your left hand.

2. Take four running stitches, so there are four "bumps" on the needle. End the needle under the ribbon. Pull the needle and thread through and go back down at point A. By going back into A, the gathered ribbon will cluster into a small flower.

3. Make a Slip Knot on the back side to hold the flower in place. Hold the remaining ribbon flat and come up in the middle ¼" away from the flower. Proceed to make the next flower.

RUTH'S RUCHED RIBBON

Here is one of my favorite stitches taught to me by Ruth Stonely of Brisbane, Australia. Not only is she an internationally known quilt artist, she is also a wonderful teacher. The ribbon can meander along crazy quilt seams, be worked in circles for flowers, or act as filler for garden scenes.

TIP
Sometimes I just alternate from inside edge to inside edge. Treat these two ribbons as one, and follow the same steps as for a single ribbon. (This effect is much fuller and more uneven, which makes it very good for texture.)

1.
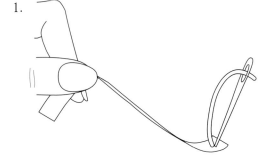

2.
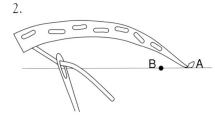

3.
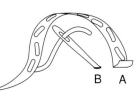

4.
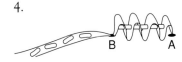

5.

6.
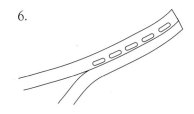

1. Thread a fine needle with a smooth metallic thread. Choose a long length of 4mm or wider silk ribbon.

2. Anchor the silk ribbon firmly to the fabric with the thread. Make a Slip Knot on the back side of the fabric and come back up with the metallic thread. Hold the ribbon in your free hand. Take large, uneven running stitches in the middle of the ribbon. (Ruth insists that the sloppier the stitches, the better the ruching looks!) End with the needle under the ribbon. You should have 3" to 4" of running stitches.

3. Go into the fabric about ½" from the anchored end. Pull gently and the ribbon will gather up into the ½" space.

4. Come back up in the center of the ribbon and continue to make 3" to 4" of running stitches. Again, end under the ribbon and sew it ½" from point B. Use the point of the needle to arrange the gathers. Depending on the amount of running stitches and the width of the ribbon, the gathers can be very loose or tight!

5. For a fuller look and more contrast, try using two 4mm silk ribbons laid side by side. A second ribbon can be added into a single line of ruched ribbon. Simply anchor the second ribbon into the desired area and hold the two ribbons in your free hand.

6. Make sure they overlap just slightly on the inside edges. Now take large, uneven running stitches along those overlapped edges.

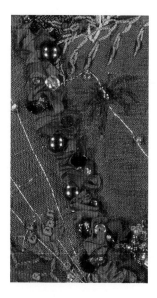

SHEER RIBBON LEAF

This technique adds a very arty and dimensional look to a project. Use sheer, wide ribbon or fabric.

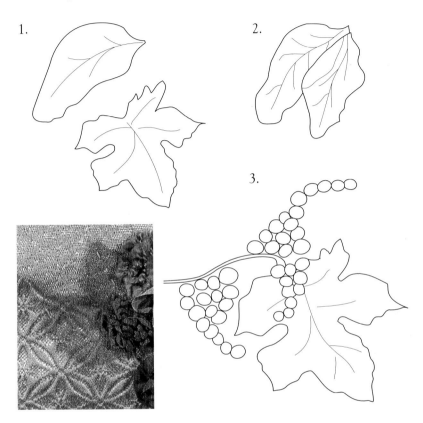

1. Trace the leaf shape onto the ribbon and cut it out. Hold the leaf to a candle flame and singe the edges.

2. Lay the leaf in place and embroider the veins using Outline or Running Stitches.

3. Once the leaf is anchored down with the stitching, work flowers on top.

SIDE RIBBON STITCH

Very similar to the Japanese Ribbon Stitch, but here the ribbon is pierced at the end on the side of the ribbon instead of in the center. This stitch can be a petal or a leaf or used side-by-side to form a larger leaf or petal.

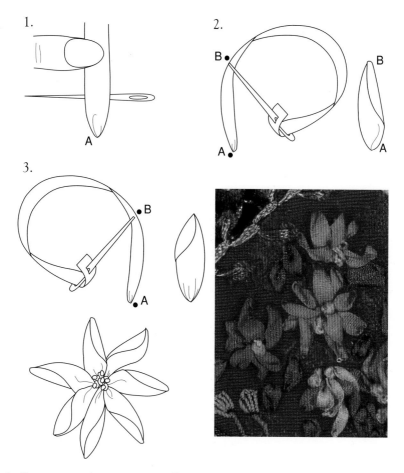

1. Come up at A using 4mm silk ribbon (or wider). Slip the needle under the ribbon while holding the ribbon in place. Slide the needle down under the ribbon to flatten. Decide on the length of the stitch and which way the tip will curve.

2. If it is pierced on the left side, the right side will curl in.

3. If pierced on the right side, the left side will curl in.

STAB STITCH

This is a single, spaced stitch worked in a regular or irregular pattern. The stitch width can vary, but do not make them too long or too loose.

1.
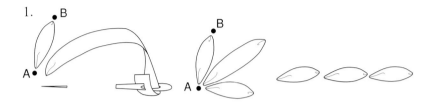

1. Come up at A and slide the needle under the ribbon to smooth it; go down at B. Make sure the ribbon lies flat and is not twisted.

TUBE ROSE

A soft, lovely curled rose that can be made in clusters.

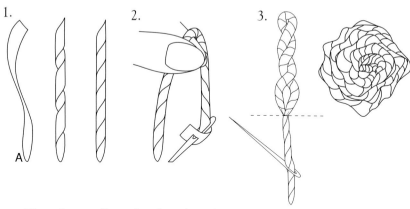

Thread a needle with a fine thread to match the color of the ribbon. Make a firm knot and set aside. Cut a 14" length of 4mm-wide ribbon and thread on a chenille needle.

1. Come up at A. Hold the needle and ribbon perpendicular to the fabric. Twist the ribbon into a tightly twisted tube. Make sure there are no loose areas.

2. Hold the tube securely in the center with your free hand. Fold it in half. Insert the needle until only the eye is above the fabric.

3. Let go of the ribbon, allowing the two halves to twist around each other to form one large tube. Gently pull down and continue pulling until the rose is the desired size. You now have a choice: you can continue to make more roses and then go back with the previously threaded needle to secure the roses with tiny stitches in the centers; or, you can make one rose at a time, securing each rose as you work.

TWISTED RIBBON STITCH

An excellent stitch for spider mums or twisted seed pods. Can be twisted tightly and laid side-by-side or layered for extra fullness to act as a filler stitch. Wonderful for seaweed.

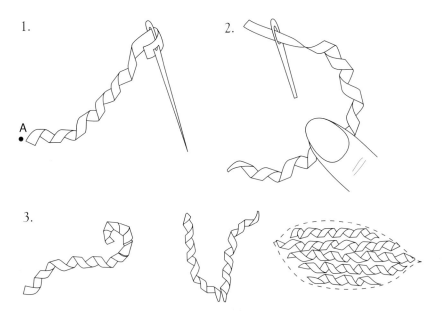

1. Come up at A. Decide on the length of the stitch. Twist the ribbon to the desired tightness.

2. Keeping the tension to hold the twists, go down and pull through.

3. Nudge the twisted ribbon into place.

VICTORIAN VELVET PANSIES

Years ago I bought a pillow top from one of my favorite antique stores, "Apples of Gold." It was a black silk square covered with 30 different velvet pansies. I've used them on many projects and for book covers, but more than that, I've enjoyed making them.

1. Choose a low-nap velvet or a panné velvet ribbon or fabric. Cut the petal shapes (they can be painted later for more detail). Back the petal pieces with fusible web. (I iron them to muslin and work each pansy as a separate unit, or you may use a glue stick to hold the petals in place on your project.)

2. Place the pieces in order from 1 to 4, securing each petal piece in place with tight Buttonhole Stitches.

3. Keep the Buttonhole Stitches very close and vary the lengths to give a more painterly look to the petals. It is not necessary to stitch the portions that will overlap. (The dashed lines on the pattern pieces indicate where Buttonhole Stitches should be worked.)

4. Work the highlighted Straight Stitches, then the very fine, wispy, center Straight Stitches and last, add the center. Then add the very fine wispy petal Straight Stitches on petals 1, 3, and 4.

ACTUAL SIZE PATTERN PIECES

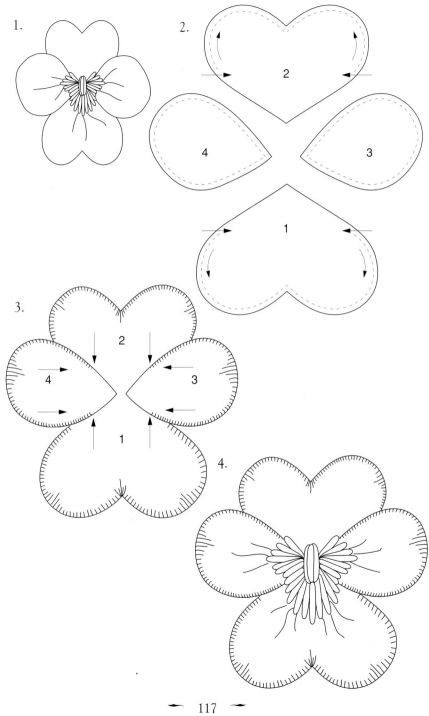

1.

2.

2

4

3

1

3.

2

4

3

1

4.

MONTANO KNOT

Uses two to three shades of color and is designed for a cascading effect. These glorified French Knots are loose and effective for filling in and for floral sprays. Depending on the size desired, they vary from one to six twists. Always start with the largest number of wraps first, decreasing by one for each knot that follows. Repeat the process with each shade of ribbon.

1. 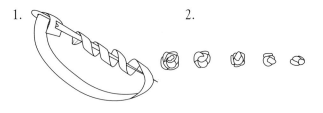 2.

1. Bring the needle up from the back and circle the ribbon around the needle (six, five, four, three, two, or one time). Hold the ribbon very loosely and do not hold the ribbon off to one side. Insert the needle back into the fabric as close to the starting point as possible.

2. Do not pull tight; let the knot remain loose and flowery.

CRAZY-QUILT
COMBINATIONS

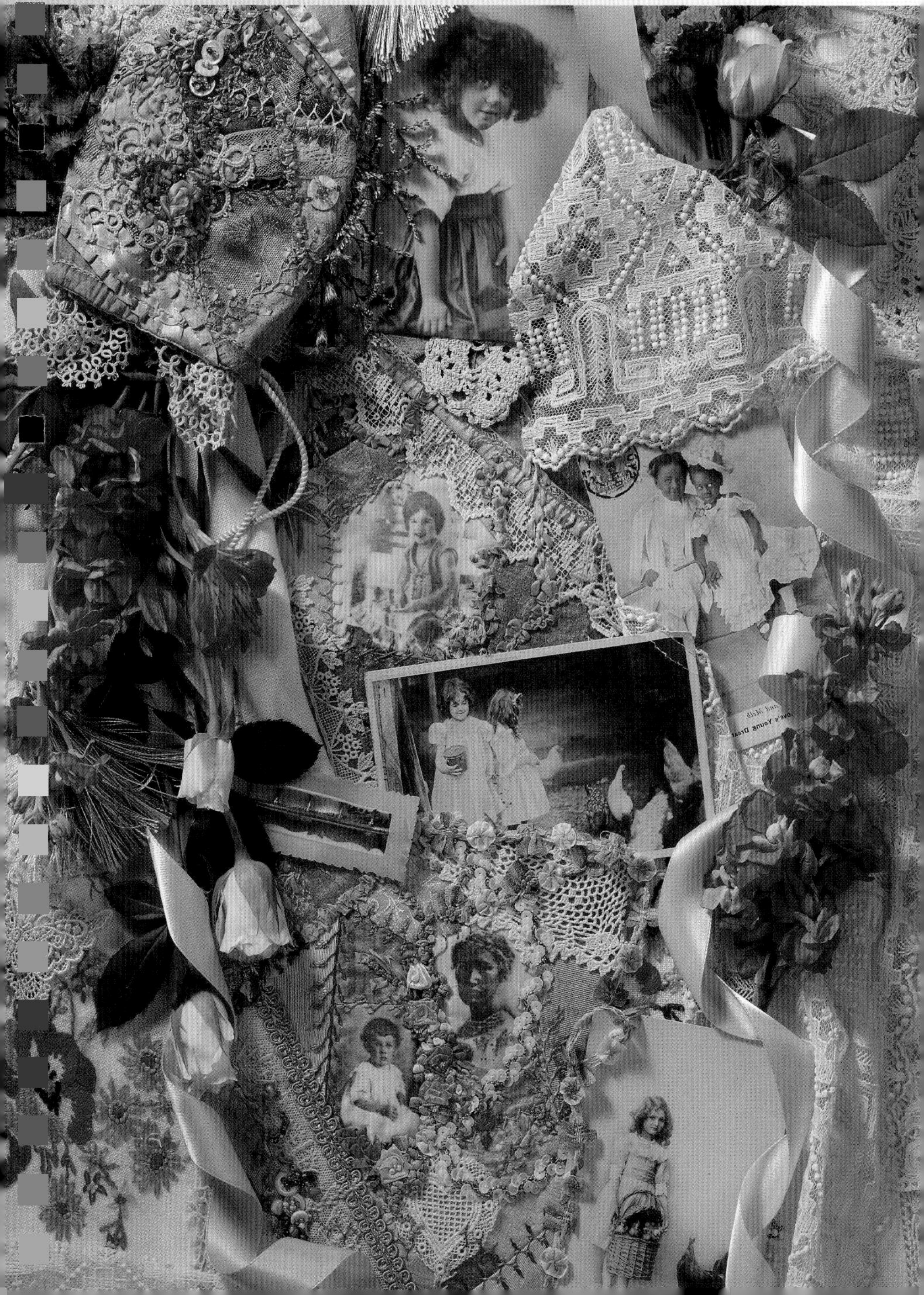

The following crazy quilt stitches all are floral designs. Most of the patterns tend to twine and undulate along the seam lines, making a more open design. Imagine these as stems, flowers, and leaves when you execute these patterns, and you will be thrilled with the results.

BUTTONHOLE STITCH VARIATIONS

Buttonhole
+
French Knot
+
Straight Stitch

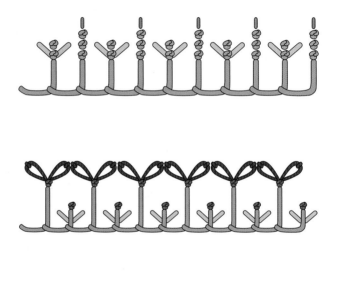

Tall & Short
Buttonhole
+
French Knot
+
Lazy Daisy
+
Straight Stitch

Pyramid
Buttonhole
+
French Knot
+
Lazy Daisy
+
Straight Stitch

Buttonhole
+
French Knot
+
Lazy Daisy

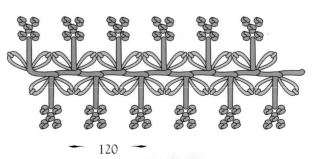

Curved Buttonhole
+
Lazy Daisy
+
French Knot

Curved Buttonhole
+
Colonial Knot
+
Lazy Daisy

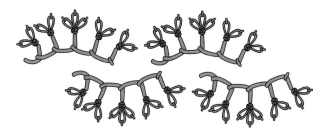

Curved Buttonhole
+
Colonial Knot

Buttonhole
+
Straight Stitch
+
Lazy Daisy
+
Colonial Knot

Curved Buttonhole
+
Colonial Knot
+
Lazy Daisy

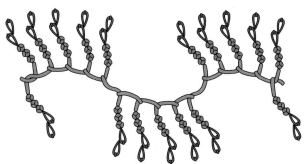

CHAIN STITCH VARIATIONS

Chain Stitch
+
Colonial Knot
+
Lazy Daisy

Chain Stitch
+
French Knot

Chain Stitch
+
French Knot
+
Lazy Daisy

Chain Stitch
+
French Knot
+
Lazy Daisy

Chain Stitch
+
French Knot

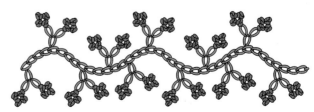

Chain Stitch
+
French Knot
+
Straight Stitch

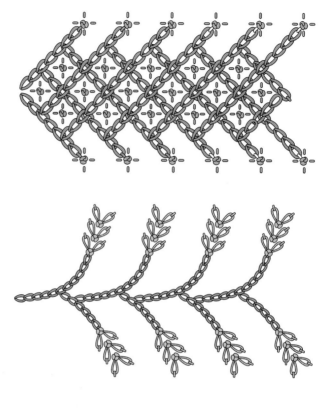

Chain Stitch
+
Colonial Knot
+
Lazy Daisy

Chain Stitch
+
Straight Stitch
+
French Knot

Chain Stitch
+
French Knot
+
Lazy Daisy

CRETAN STITCH VARIATIONS

Cretan Stitch
+
French Knot
+
Lazy Daisy
+
Straight Stitch

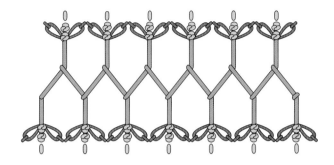

Cretan Stitch
+
French Knot
+
Lazy Daisy

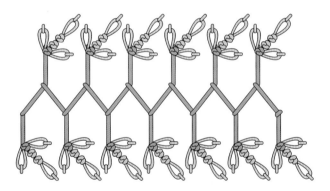

Cretan Stitch
+
Lazy Daisy
+
French Knot

Pyramid Cretan
Stitch
+
French Knot
+
Lazy Daisy

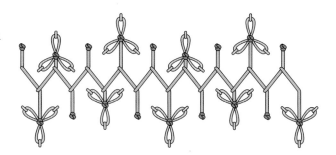

Cretan Stitch
+
Colonial Knot
+
Lazy Daisy
+
Straight Stitch

Slanted Cretan
Stitch
+
Straight Stitch
+
Colonial Knot
+
Lazy Daisy

Pyramid Cretan
+
Colonial Knot
+
Lazy Daisy
+
Straight Stitch

FAN VARIATIONS

Lazy Daisy
+
Stem Stitch
+
Colonial Knot

Lazy Daisy
+
Colonial Knot
+
Stem Stitch

Lazy Daisy with
Long Catch Stitch
+
French Knot
+
Straight Stitch

Pistil Stitch
+
Colonial Knot
+
Straight Stitch

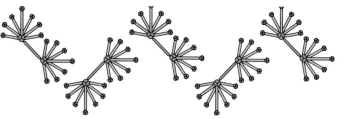

Lazy Daisy
+
Colonial Knot
+
Straight Stitch
+
Pistil Stitch

FEATHER STITCH VARIATIONS

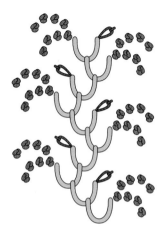

Double Feather Stitch
+
Lazy Daisy

Double Feather Stitch
+
French Knot
+
Lazy Daisy

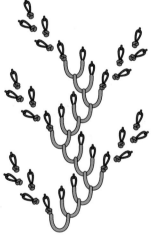

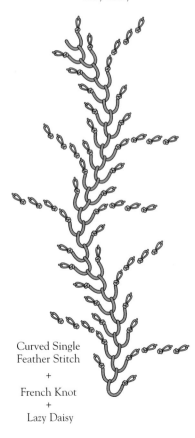

Triple Feather Stitch
+
Lazy Daisy
+
French Knot or Beads

Curved Single
Feather Stitch
+
French Knot
+
Lazy Daisy

Single Feather
Stitch
+
French Knot
or Beads

Chain Stitch
+
Single Feather
Stitch
+
Colonial Knot
+
Lazy Daisy

Feather Stitch
+
Lazy Daisy
+
Colonial Knot

HERRINGBONE VARIATIONS

Herringbone
+
Straight Stitch
+
Lazy Daisy
+
French Knot

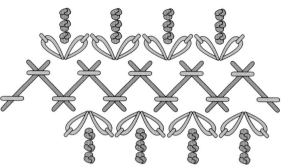

Herringbone
+
Straight Stitch
+
Lazy Daisy
+
Colonial Knot

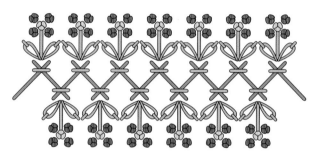

Herringbone
+
Straight Stitch
+
Lazy Daisy
+
French Knot

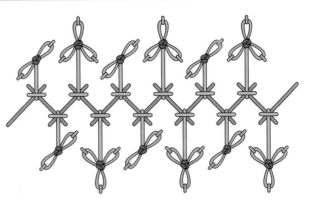

Herringbone
+
Straight Stitch
+
Lazy Daisy
+
French Knot

LAZY DAISY VARIATIONS

Long & Medium
Lazy Daisy
+
Colonial Knot

Long & Medium
Lazy Daisy
+
Straight Stitch

Long & Short
Lazy Daisy
+
Pistil Stitch
+
Colonial Knot

Long & Short
Lazy Daisy
+
Straight Stitch
+
Pistil Stitch
+
Stem Stitch
+
French Knot

Long Lazy Daisy
with Long
Catch Stitch

+

Pistil Stitch

+

Colonial Knot

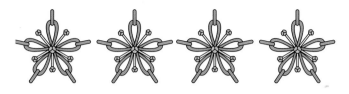

Short Lazy Daisy

+

French Knot

Long & Short
Lazy Daisy

+

Outline Stitch

+

Pistil Stitch

+

French Knot

Lazy Daisy

+

French Knot
or Beads

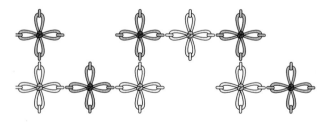

Lazy Daisy

+

French Knot

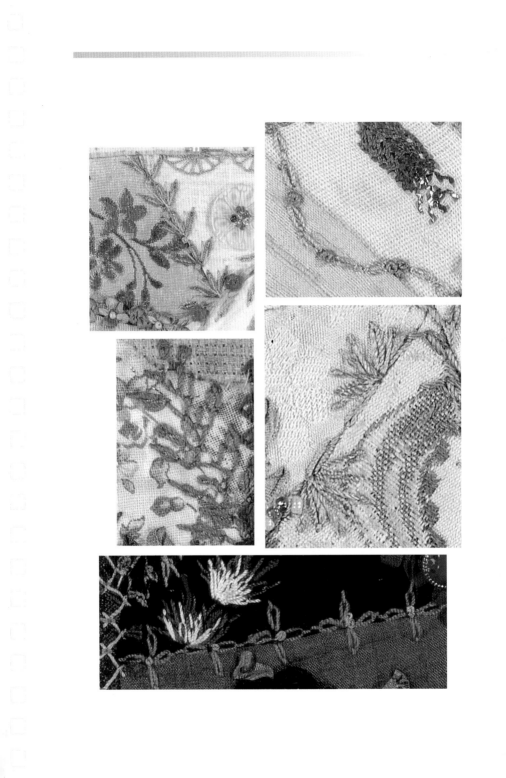

VINE VARIATIONS

Chain Stitch or Stem Stitch
+
Lazy Daisy
+
Colonial Knot
+
French Knot

Lazy Daisy with
Long Catch Stitch
+
Colonial Knot
+
Single Wrap French Knot
+
Chain Stitch
+
Outline Stitch

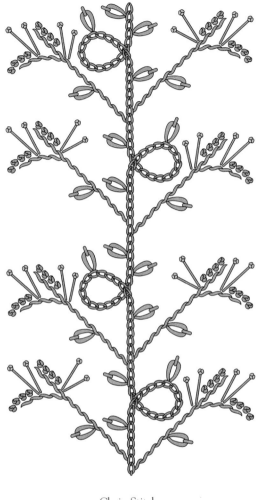

Chain Stitch
+
Stem Stitch
+
Lazy Daisy
+
Colonial Knot
+
French Knot
+
Pistil Stitch
+
Straight Stitch

Chain Stitch
+
French Knot
+
Lazy Daisy
+
Pistil Stitch
+
Outline Stitch

Chain Stitch
+
French Knot
+
Straight Stitch

Decorated Lazy Daisy
+
Straight Stitch
+
Chain Stitch

SEMICIRCLE VARIATIONS

Outline Stitch
+
Straight Stitch
+
Colonial Knot
+
Lazy Daisy

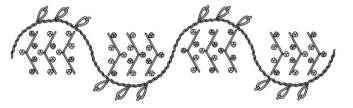

Chain Stitch
+
Lazy Daisy

Fly Stitch
+
French Knot

Maidenhair
Stitch
+
Single Wrap
French Knot

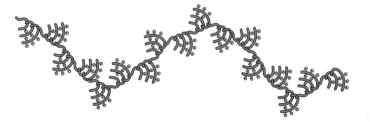

ZIGZAGS & SQUARES

Straight Stitch
+
Lazy Daisy
+
French Knot

Straight Stitch
+
Lazy Daisy
+
French Knot

Straight Stitch
+
Long & Short
Lazy Daisy
+
French Knot

Rosette Stitch
+
Lazy Daisy
+
Straight Stitch

Straight Stitch
+
Lazy Daisy
+
Colonial Knot

RIBBON AND THREAD VARIATIONS

Ruth's Rosettes

+

Straight Stitch
(ribbon)

+

Japanese Ribbon
Stitch (ribbon)

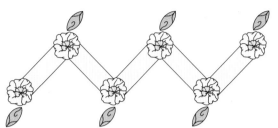

Ruth's Rosettes

+

Straight Stitch
(ribbon)

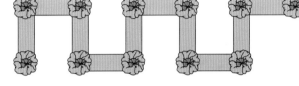

Double Feather
Stitch (thread)

+

Short Japanese
Ribbon Stitch
(ribbon)

+

French Knot
(ribbon) or Beads

Double Feather Stitch (thread)
+
Colonial Knot (ribbon)
+
Japanese Ribbon Stitch (ribbon)

Triple Feather Stitch (thread)
+
Decorated Lazy Daisy (ribbon)
+
Japanese Ribbon Stitch (ribbon)

Double Feather Stitch (thread)
+
Padded Rosebud (ribbon)
+
Colonial Knot (ribbon)

FREE-FORM
EMBROIDERY

FREE-FORM EMBROIDERY

I love working with floral designs because they please me both visually and spiritually. Over the years I have developed the confidence to think like a painter with fabric, threads, and ribbons. Whether I am designing art for wearable garments, accessories, crazy quilts, or land-or seascapes, what always appears in my work are flowers. The following needleart collages are laid out from start to finish so that you can follow the process.

Although my work seems to be very free and easy, I do have a set process from which I seldom vary. No matter how hard I try to leave out a few steps, I always regret it, and it creates more problems. Over the years I have wasted more time waiting for inspiration to come up with a good design or idea, and it wasn't until I started to keep an art journal and store clippings that I realized inspiration is 90% research!

I recommend having a definite idea, along with colored drawings, to start the plan for your project. Know the exact size of your finished project beforehand, so there will be no surprises. Before you ever set needle to thread, be sure you have all your materials at hand. There is nothing worse than being in the middle of a creative streak and then having to stop and search for that special thread or button. By having a sketch and notes on the project, you will have an idea of what materials to pull. (Perhaps you won't use them all, and there will certainly be extras you will need, but the majority will be at hand.)

Remember to think like a painter, and that all your projects are a backward journey. You have to start at the furthest point and work forward. Yes, some of your stitches will get covered up but that is part of the process...building forward. I hope you enjoy the following projects and that you will try some of them. Above all relax and enjoy!

CRAZY-QUILT COLLAGE

Crazy quilting is my first love, and I enjoy the challenges it offers. Some people think that everything and anything goes into a crazy quilt and that it must be very easy, but this method of needlework offers a much larger challenge and is the most painterly method of quilting. Because there are no patterns or templates and because the maker must think like a painter, crazy quilting can be quite daunting.

Crazy quilting is very process-oriented, yet once you work through the stages it becomes second nature. And once you learn to think like a painter, everything from clothing design to quilting will seem a little easier. Read through the "Thinking Like A Painter" section (page 13) to refresh your memory.

This crazy-quilt collage is filled with floral ribbons, trim, and stitches to give you ideas for your own projects. After carefully choosing my fabrics (I had to decide if it would be a pastel, dusty, or a jewel-tone collage), I checked once again to make sure that no one fabric bounced forward too fast; in other words, that it was not too light for the project. You want the fabrics to be complementary colors and to sparkle when used against each other. Make sure that you have a good variety of solids, patterns, and textured fabrics in an equal amount of cool and warm tones. These fabrics represent the first colorwash and will act as a background for the embellishments. Remember that you will be layering ribbons, laces, and many needlework techniques over this background.

For this piece I tried to keep a floral theme right down to the Victorian stitches which you can find in the Crazy-Quilt Combination section.

Bird
Cherry.

grapes

COTONE

Snow berries

Black
Berries

Asiatic Sweet Leaf

STITCHES FOR
BERRIES....
French KNOT
COLONIAL KNOT
SATIN STITCH
Chinese KNOT
MONTANO KNOT
Chain STITCH
Long & short
STRaight
Stitch.

Hawthorn

Raspberry

J.B.N.

IF....you can't be a
good example, Then
you'll just have To be
a horrible warning!....
Catherine Aird.

HANGING BASKET

I like to use watercolors to create interesting backgrounds, and I had worked up several pieces. But it wasn't until I was visiting Victoria, British Columbia, Canada that I found the perfect subject to use with the watercolor backgrounds. It was summer, and everywhere I looked there were beautiful hanging baskets, cascading from walls, lamp posts, windows, and fences. I made several sketches and rushed home to work the designs that could be used on the painted backgrounds.

The focus of this piece is the flower basket, so the background has to act as subtle shadows and should suggest shapes. With watercolors, I washed in several colors to complement the flowers in the basket. I then blocked in the area of the basket and the greenery. Next I used several pieces of organza to suggest the moss basket and tacked them in place.

Using the process of background, midground, and foreground (page 13) I worked in the flowers and greenery...making sure to use small fine stitches in the back, getting them larger as I moved forward.

With a piece like this it is hard to stop! I had to remove several stitches because the painted background shape was completely covered! I have drawn hanging baskets (page 152) for you to use as backgrounds for your needlework. Enlarge them and trace the designs to fabric. Keep your watercolors soft to act as a background and enhance your embroidery.

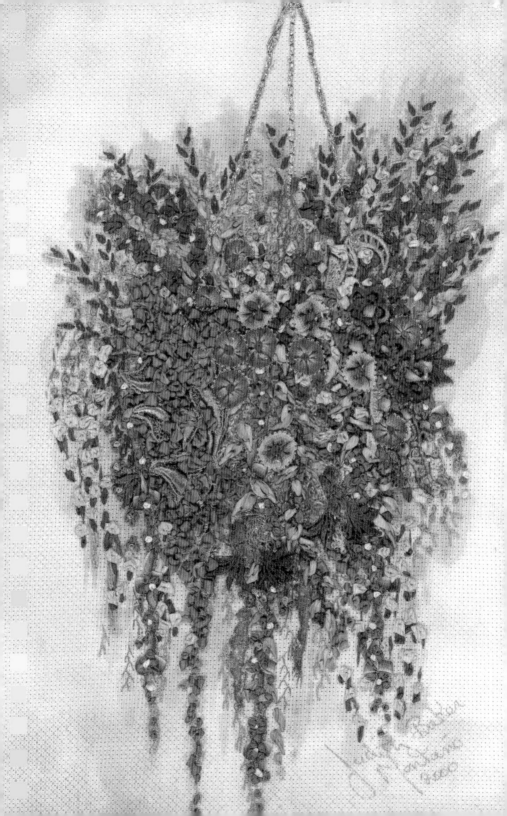

Ferns...
- Wheat ear
- Fly Stitch
- Feather Stitch
- Van Dyke St.

Alyssium...
- French Knots
- granitos
Lobelia...
- Chinese Knot
- Colonial Knots

Basket o 'gold...
- Colonial Knots
- French Knots

Impatiens...
- Loop Stitch

Trailing Petunia...
- Ribbon Side St.
- Triangle button hole shapes...

Verbina...
- French Knots

Trailing Geranium...
- Loop Stitch
Colonial Knots

Ferns...
- Fern Stitch
- Plume Stitch
- Fish bone St.

Hanging baskets are perfect for floral collages on painted backgrounds. Paint the baskets in loose shapes of color.... Work detail in with Threads and Ribbon.

Hanging Baskets Always
bring back Memories of VicTORia,
British Columbia in Spring
and Tea at The
EMPRESS Hotel
with
Uncle Chris.....

MONTANO
KNOT.

good Trailing STiTches:
French KNOTS....
colonial KNOTS ...
MONTaNO KNOT...

BULLioN..
whip STiTch:

DOWN-UNDER IN COLORADO

Years ago I purchased a dilapidated 1885 cottage that was home to a skunk, several bats, and a battalion of field mice. I spent my free time in an ancient mobile home, just behind the apple trees, daydreaming about restoring the cottage. The old cottage was voted the ugliest house in town, and it was the opinion of the town elders that only a bulldozer could put it out of its misery!

Over the last twelve years on my Australian tours, I admired the way the Australians restored and maintained their old properties. While comparing some of the cottages, I realized that many of the Aussie houses looked like my old Colorado cottage. What a stroke of luck! I might not be able to live full-time in Australia, but I found I could bring Australia home.

After months and months of research and careful planning, the restoration took place. I now have an Australian cottage, complete with a tin roof and wooden awnings carved with kangaroos and emus! My family is thrilled to have a Colorado retreat that will bring joy for generations to come. The towns people now say we have the sweetest home in town, and they are thrilled that we have saved the old girl.

I decided to commemorate our little cottage in fabric and needlework. I started by collecting solid blue fabrics, with a bit of turquoise hue that resembles the Colorado sky. Next I gathered all types of small floral prints for the foreground and garden area. I decided on a horizontal layout of 11" by 14", as this would give me more room for embellishment.

I had a photograph of the cottage enlarged at a copy center. I then traced the scene to tissue paper and then to watercolor paper.

By outlining with black ink and filling in with colored pencils, I chose the colors for the garden area. I then traced the cottage onto 18-count Aida cloth. After completing the crazy quilt surround, I carefully cut out the opening and burned the edges to give the effect of a drawn edge. Aligning the surround and the Aida cloth, I sewed them both into place.

Next, I used watercolors to paint the sky, trees, and shrub shapes, making sure they spread into the crazy-quilt surround. Working from the sky downward, I added the Victorian stitches. In the sky area, I used fine, similar colored threads. In the garden, I used bright floral colors, working larger stitches as I got to the bottom.

Once again, I start anew in the background to create a sense of depth. All the stitches are very fine and very small so they look far away. As I worked forward the stitches got larger, and the threads and ribbon are heavier. Once in the foreground I finish by adding buttons, beads, and more detail.

Old houses have a history
a story to tell
Some good - Some bad.
but always a story
We just have to lis'n

It was love at first sight.
Every one thought I was Crazy
When I bought the derelict old cottage
but I could see her beauty
I could hear the story..

Now lovingly resto'd
"The Old Carver Place"
sits among greener'
and flowers.
Decked in riotous
color, trims from Austr'
stain glass from England,
bits and bobs from
Canada....
Filled with light, moment'
of travel, the chatter of
family and friends - th'
Slightly off key music of life ∞∞

The old cottage adds another chapter to
her story.

Judith 1999.

Just outside of Geneva, across the field from Aunt Bessie's house was a marvelous old cottage with a stone courtyard.

Hollyhocks call out "grandma, apple pie, Tea and scones.... Cottage gate.....

Button hole Hollyhocks..

Fox glove detached chain →

Cottage roses can be worked in colonial knots and Fargo stitches.... Straight stitch leaves

delphiniums - .... Montano Knots or French knot stitches work well.... Curled leaf stitches.

159 - 159 -

UNDERWATER GARDEN

At the age of fifty I decided to overcome my fear of water. I took classes on scuba diving and snorkeling in Australia—and I have never been the same since diving at the Great Barrier reef. I was able to glide among coral gardens filled with glorious color, and a whole new world opened up to me.

I keep trying to reproduce underwater gardens in needlework. In an underwater scene, you can use vivid color and create whimsical shapes that would never appear above ground. I have discovered that by using sheer overlays I can create a feeling of depth in my underwater scenes. For this project, I used a painted background as well as burned-edge sheers to evoke a feeling of mystery. I was able to slip threads in behind the sheers to indicate coral and seaweed.

Once again the same rules apply to the underwater scenes: form a background, midground, and a foreground. Darks recede and lights come forward. Under water you have valleys, hills, flat areas, and cliffs...the only difference is that the light source comes only from above!

Under water gardens vary a bit
From the gardens on Land
eg.
1. The Light source is directly
over head
2. The Tides and currents dictate
any Movement.
They are the same in that:
1. There is a background,
Midground and Foreground
2. There is a horizon, with
hills, valleys and cliffs
3. All the rules of Landscape
apply to under water gardens!
4. Under water Flowers are
Made up of Coral, sea Anenomes
and sea weed.

Here's To The Little clown Fish who Protects his Patch of anenome even against divers who must look like a submarine To him!!

Being a Pisces I love The water.... As a child, in land in Alberta Canada, I used To dream about the ocean, upon my First visit I was not disapointed! I return at least once a year.

ART NOUVEAU LADY

Kathryn and Judith of Adelaide, Australia produce copyright-free antique pictures onto silk. I admire their work and consider them my good friends. This lovely *Art Nouveau Lady* just called to me, and I was able to incorporate a Victorian silk, floral appliqué into the piece along with silk ribbon and threads.

I used Zwicki® silk six-stranded threads in the background and midground. The beauty of stranded thread is that it can be used as one strand for fine work, and up to all the strands for heavier foreground work.

The chrysanthemums in the foreground are worked with 4mm silk ribbon using the Twisted Ribbon Stitch (page 115.) My challenge on this piece was to keep my colors soft and muted to give a feeling of age (use the Montano Color chart, page 15). By working in light-to-medium dusty hues, so as not to overpower the design, I think this turned out well.

While at the Crazy-Quilt Convention I learned a British color photocopy transfer method.

Collect a medium-size jar with a lid, a 2" paint brush, mineral spirits (paint thinner), cotton balls, dishwashing liquid, smooth fabric with a tight weave, a color copy with intensified color, an iron and a hard surface (cookie sheet or butcher block).

COLOR TRANSFER METHOD: Work in a well-ventilated room. Fill the jar half way with water and add the thinner to make it ¾ full. Add a small squirt of the detergent. Put the lid on and shake gently until it's well mixed. Paint the mixture onto the front and back of the copy... if the ink smears then paint only the back. Saturate the paper; then set it aside for five minutes. Set the iron at a high heat. Lay the fabric face-up on the hard surface, and lay the copy face down on the fabric. Lay a piece of white paper on the silk and iron with the hot iron. (Be sure to keep the iron moving.) Lift a corner to see if it is transferring...if not keep ironing for a few more minutes.

Lilla Le Vine, who wrote *Ribbon Works Special Edition*, suggests using a sheet of aluminum foil. Fold the foil in half, sandwiching the fabric and photocopy between the sheets, and then iron it with a hot iron. I have tried both ways with great success.

Reach high,
For Stars Lie
hidden in your soul.
Dream deep,
For every dream
precedes The goal.
...Pamela
Vaul
Starr.

ART Nouveau
1890 - 1914
A style or Movement in which
ART and Life were The same,
Nature, history and Symbolism were
Meshed into ART Nouveau
Romantic, Sensual, Flowing Lines

The Iris is such
a stately Flower,
so elegant and so
reserved..... rather
haughty.....
I once knew an
Irish girl with Flame
red hair, by The name
of Iris....

Unlike her
Floral counter-
part, Iris had
a twinkle in her
eye, loved a
good joke and
was a lot
more Fun!!

J.B.M.

elinor peace bailey

One spring day in Colorado, I was feeling sorry for myself over an impending book deadline. I wanted to be out in my garden! A package arrived and upon opening it, out fell two antique crazy quilt squares and a painting-on-velvet of a little girl. The note read "When I saw these I thought of you—love, elinor." She had done it again… elinor peace bailey—dollmaker, designer, poet, singer extraordinare, and mentor—had made me happy! The piece with the little girl was obviously very old and fragile, and I kept her in my studio until I could use her to create something special.

I finally decided to surround the little girl in a bower of lace and flowers that would remind me of special friends. I added paint and tea-dyed lace. Then I added the branches with Feather Stitches, Portuguese Stem Stitches, and String of Pearls. To these I added dozens of Mokuba Flowers plus spikes of Joyce (Fargo) Flowers.

From an afternoon lesson with my sister Karen and with her help, I was able to add Elly's Wire Ribbon Pansies, plus some Victorian Velvet Pansies. Nestled among the bower are sprays of Tube Roses, and Jan's and Helen's Antique Roses and buds. I enjoyed this project so much that I didn't want it to end. It now hangs in our Colorado cottage for everyone to enjoy. This piece brings a smile to my face every time I pass by.

Upon creating elinor Peace bailey
God Tripped and dropped The mold
shattering it into pieces!
which is a great pity
because he never created
another woman Like her!

elinor is Compassionate
with a keen intellect
and a marvelous sense of humor.
The creator gave her great
Talents in music, prose and art.
Above all he made her a Teacher
so all could learn From her
even if only in her presence.
God bless elinor peace!

The act of Longing
For something
Will always be more intense
Than the requiring of it.
ooooo gail Godwin.

SHANTZIE'S GARDEN

I never work in my garden without thinking of my Grandma Shantz. In fact, her tombstone reads "Your Garden is My Memory." She lived in a small house with the traditional 50 by 150 foot yard. Besides a huge vegetable garden in the back, her pride and joy was her perennial flower garden. I can still see her puttering among those gorgeous flowers. I wrote *Recollections* with her in mind, and even now I just have to look out to my garden, and she's with me. She has passed her "green thumb" to me and my sisters, and we can cheerfully talk for hours about gardening.

For this project, I dyed the background, creating a "background, midground, and foreground." I tried to imagine what was behind the fence, and with fine threads I worked Feather Stitches, String of Pearls, and Straight Stitches.

The fence came next with Ribbon Split Stitches for posts and couched silk threads. When the fence was completed, I marched a row of perennials along it. Starting with Circle Buttonholes for hollyhocks, and Straight Stitches and Open-Ended Lazy Daisies for iris, I added French Knots for delphinium, Stab Stitches for lily buds, and Triangle Buttonholes for foxglove.

For the rose trellis, I couched down heavy variegated silk threads, and embroidered Chain Stitches along with Fargo Flower roses. It was so much fun to do that I had to work hard not to fill in every space!

Through the midground, I made Lazy Daisy Stitches plus Bullion Stitches to indicate hydrangea and other bulb flowers. Down in the foreground I was able to add lavender with Bullion and String of Pearl stitches plus phlox worked in a ribbon Loop Stitch. In front are Circle Buttonhole hollyhocks and foxgloves made from Judith's Curled Leaf stitches. Crosshatches of Fly Stitches add a suggestion of texture to the walkway. Use the many ideas in the Botanical Shapes section to create your own plant shapes and for new ideas.

garden plants come i
all sorts of shapes a !
sizes .... a good varie
make for an interest g
garden....

Mat- Forming
(Soapwort)
Forms a dense ground
cover. Flower above The Matt.

Prostrate
(Ice plant)
Stems spread out over
The ground.
Flowers close to The
Foliage

Cushion or Mound-Forming
(Cushion Spurge)
Forms a low clump
Tightly packed stems....

Spreading (Lavender)
Curves upward in a densley
packed mass.

Erect (Cone Flower)
upright stems
support Leaves
and Flowers

Climbing
and Scandent
(grape vine)
Long Flexible stems
That must be Supported

Clump Forming
(Delphinium)
Flower stems
and Leaves Form
dense mound.

Stemless —
Flowers rise on
Tall stems above
The Leaves.

Judith Baker Montano

Before
Visiting my GRANDMA
HANTZ... We had to STOP
at The barn For a gunny
Sack of horse Manure! She
Would soak it in a rain barrel
To make Manure Tea for her garden.
She was The only grandmother
I've ever known to preFer Horse
Manure To candy and perfume!!
I loved her so much...
She was a survivor - a real
Character... when I'm in my
garden... She's always with me
whispering "Don't Forget The Tea."

A HORSE! A HORSE!
My garden For
A Horse!!

BIBLIOGRAPHY

1. *A-Z Encyclopedia of Garden Plants*....Brickel and Zuk, Editors
   DK Publishing, Inc., New York, NY, 1997
2. *An Encyclopedia of Ribbon Embroidery Flowers*...Deanna Hall West, ASN
   Publishing, San Marcos, CA, 1995
3. *An Encyclopedia of Wool Embroidery*....Merilyn Hazelwood
   Merriwood Press, Tasmania, Australia, 1997
4. *Australian Wild Flowers*....Michael Morcombe
   Summet Books, Dee Whey West, Australia, 1970
5. *Creative Hand Embroidery*....Sue Newhouse
   Search Press, Turnbridge Wells, Kent, England, 1993
6. *Desert Wild Flowers*....Arizona Native Plant Society
   Arizona Native Plant Society, Tucson, Arizona
7. *Embroidered Flowers*.....Pamela Watts
   B.T. Batsford Ltd., London, England, 1995
8. *Embroidery From the Garden*.....Diana Lampe
   Sally Milner Publishing, Bura Creek, NSW, Australia, 1997
9. *Fabric Painting for Embroidery*.....Valerie Campbell-Harding
   Sterling Publishing Co., London, England, 1990
10. *Gardens In Embroidery*.....Val Holms
    B.T. Batsford, London, England, 1991
11. *Ribbon Basics*.....Mary Jo Hiney and Joy Anckner
    Sterling Publishing Co., New York, NY, 1995
12. *Ribbon Works Special Edition Featuring Lilla Le Vine*....Lilla Le Vine
    Ribbon Works Special Edition, Gladewater, Texas, 1998 pg 28
13. *The Art of Embroidery*......Julia Barton
    Merehurst Press, London, England, 1989
14. *The Art of the Needle*.......Jan Beaney
    Century Hutchinson Ltd., London, England, 1983
15. *The Complete Handbook of Garden Plants*.....Michael Wright
    Penguin Books, London, England, 1984
16. *The Rose Bible*.....Rayford Clayton Reddell
    Chronicle Press, San Francisco, CA, 1998
17. *The Merehurst Book of Needlework*....Diana Brinnon...editor
    Merehurst Ltd., London, England, 1993
18. *Treasury of Flower Designs* ......Susan Gaber
    Dover Publications, Inc, New York, NY, 1981
19. *Wild Flowers*.....Rick Imes
    Rodale Press, Emmaus, PA, 1992